Authentic Relationships in Group Care for Infants and Toddlers – Resources for Infant Educarers (RIE) Principles into Practice

Edited by Stephanie Petrie and Sue Owen

Jessica Kingsley Publishers
London and Philadelphia

First published in 2005
by Jessica Kingsley Publishers
116 Pentonville Road
London N1 9JB, UK
and
400 Market Street, Suite 400
Philadelphia, PA 19106, USA

www.jkp.com

Copyright © Jessica Kingsley Publishers 2005

Library of Congress Cataloging in Publication Data
Authentic relationships in group care for infants and toddlers - resources for infant educators (RIE) principles into practice / edited by Stephanie Petrie and Sue Owen.-- 1st American pbk. ed.
    p. cm.
Includes bibliographical references and index.
ISBN 1-84310-117-3 (pbk.)
1. Infants--Care. 2. Toddlers--Care. 3. Child care services. 4. Early childhood education. 5. Child care services--Great Britain. I. Petrie, Stephanie. II. Owen, Sue.
HQ774.A88 2005
362.7--dc22

2004019597

British Library Cataloguing in Publication Data
A CIP catalogue record for this book is available from the British Library

ISBN-13: 978 1 84310 117 8
ISBN-10: 1 84310 117 3

Printed and Bound in Great Britain by
Athenaeum Press, Gateshead, Tyne and Wear

To Sarah Petrie, who introduced me to RIE
and taught me everything I know about babies
and toddlers. Sorry for being such a slow learner!

Stephanie Petrie

For my daughter, Katharyn Owen, with love and thanks.

Sue Owen

Acknowledgments

The authors would like to thank the Gerber family for permission to use Magda Gerber's original writing; Joseph Amanzio for the photograph of Magda Gerber on page 35; Polly Elam for all other photographs; Patty Ryan, Infant Education Specialist and RIE Associate, for Figure 3.2 on page 58.

Thanks also to Ann Robinson at the National Children's Bureau for finding so many useful references for us.

Contents

Introduction   9
Stephanie Petrie, University of Liverpool and Sue Owen, National Children's Bureau

1. The Work of Emmi Pikler and Magda Gerber   17
Stephanie Petrie, University of Liverpool

2. RIE Principles and Practices   35
Magda Gerber, RIE Founding Director, Los Angeles

3. The RIE Early Years "Curriculum"   51
Ruth Money, RIE Associate

4. Using the RIE Approach in a Family Day Care Home   69
Catherine Coughlan, family day care provider

5. Creating Quality Infant Group Care Programs   83
Polly Elam, RIE Associate

6. RIE Parent–Infant Guidance Classes   93
Elizabeth Memel, RIE Associate and Lee Fernandez, child care administrator and RIE Associate

7. To Teach as Magda Taught *or* Mutual Respect and Trust: The Role of the Mentor in RIE   113
Polly Elam, RIE Associate

8. Applicability of the Pikler/Gerber Approach in the UK Context   127
Sue Owen, National Children's Bureau and Stephanie Petrie, University of Liverpool

GLOSSARY   141

REFERENCES   145

SUBJECT INDEX   151

AUTHOR INDEX   159

Introduction

Stephanie Petrie and Sue Owen

From Stephanie Petrie

When I was first told about RIE (Resources for Infant Educarers – pronounced "rye") in the early 1990s all my prejudice and bigotry came to the fore. "Oh yeah", I thought, "child care from California? What on earth have the Americans to teach us—everyone knows they have the worst-behaved children in the world!" Shortly afterwards, while on holiday in the US, I saw RIE in action in the home of a one-year-old boy. His mother and nanny had attended a RIE parent–infant course together to make sure he had continuity of care while his mum worked. Somewhat against my will I was impressed. I was impressed by the confident, relaxed baby I saw and by his relationship with his carer. All the characteristics of quality care, discussed later, were present. The child was treated respectfully, given choice, but when an adult agenda had to be paramount it was explained appropriately and his feelings were acknowledged. The most amazing thing for me, however, was his physical confidence and the degree to which he was allowed to explore his world without adult interference. His space was sufficiently safe that falling from time to time was not a big disaster but a learning experience for him. His carer reflected confidence in his ability to problem-solve and a warm word or look gave him, in turn, confidence to negotiate the terrain and physical challenges himself. It made me reflect on how I cared for my own child when she was that age. I was completely different. I anticipated disaster at every turn and was always the mother standing by the play equipment to catch my daughter in case she fell off. I gave running commentaries – "Don't do this or you'll fall," "Stay away from that, it's dangerous" and even worse "No, this is the way to play with this toy." The difference between what I did as a mother and what I observed intrigued me. I found out a little about Magda Gerber and her ideas and I wanted to learn more, although I still had many reservations. One in particular was that RIE might work for affluent parents with time and money to devote to their child but I couldn't see how hard-pressed poor and lone parents could utilize the technique.

In December 2000 I was awarded a small grant from the Dempster Bequest Fund that enabled me to travel to the US and study RIE. In January 2001 I successfully completed the ten-day intensive certificated course, RIE I Theory and Observation. This is the first part of a three stage qualifying training program currently offered by RIE, primarily in Los Angeles, although ways of offering training to those in other countries are currently being explored (for further discussion see Chapter 7 or contact RIE – see Glossary). I was able to return on several occasions to observe RIE-influenced provision, attend conferences and talk to RIE associates and practitioners. The RIE organization is a modest non-profit enterprise and apart from a small amount of clerical assistance and a full-time volunteer, all the training, publications, conferences and so on are done on a voluntary basis by people who also have full-time employment elsewhere. Many became involved with RIE through their contact with Magda Gerber, who impresses those she meets as much as her mentor, the Hungarian pediatrician Emmi Pikler had impressed her. At the time I did my training, she still attended each course to meet and talk with students, notwithstanding her considerable age. Although challenged by short-term memory loss she was able to share many wise and humane insights about children, caring and indeed the world in general and it was a privilege to meet her. However, I was a difficult and challenging student. I had many vigorous discussions with RIE associates and practitioners, particularly about the limited ways those in other countries could access training and support. I was not always sure that the full potential of the Pikler/Gerber approach was being explored with poor and young parents.

However, I *was* always impressed with the RIE-influenced provision I saw; whether in family-care or center-care, whether non-profit or commercial, whether state or federal. I began to think about the gaps in provision and services for young children and their families in the UK and how RIE could, through a shared approach, help to provide continuity for children at times of change – such as when young children spend time in day care or foster care. But RIE is of use to all parents and while I believe I was a "good enough" parent, if I had been helped to understand the cues of my own child sooner and more accurately I know that her early years, especially her early months, would have been less fraught and more enjoyable for both of us. As discussed later, reducing the difficulties facing young, poor and lone parents and their children is a UK government priority and programs such as Sure Start and Sure Start Plus have been established to support them, along with wider aims. The RIE approach not only offers parent education in a general sense but also builds the relationship between carer and child during those crucial early months. Babies who are understood better are easier to care for. Parents who are confident they can understand their babies find parenting a little less stressful and demanding.

In the summer of 2001 I visited California with my colleague Sue Owen from the National Children's Bureau in the UK, an early years specialist who, I felt, would be able to judge the RIE approach in the light of her knowledge and experience of the UK early years situation. Sue had heard of Magda Gerber and her work in the 1970s and knew of its influence in Belgium where she has close professional connections, but she had never had the opportunity to see RIE-influenced settings in practice. She also was impressed by the people we met and the settings we visited, which included a private day nursery and a large, federal child care facility. We decided that we would like to write about RIE, including the first-hand accounts of Magda Gerber and the California practitioners whom she had trained, in order to bring this approach to a wider audience that could consider its potential for work in this country. This book is the result of our enthusiasm and we are grateful to Jessica Kingsley Publishers for seeing its potential.

From Stephanie Petrie and Sue Owen

This book sets out to draw to the attention of those involved with group care for infants and young toddlers the ideas and approaches of the child care practitioners Emmi Pikler and Magda Gerber. We describe their work with infants and toddlers in Hungary and the US and the literature and research underpinning it as an introduction to a series of chapters written by contemporary practitioners from the organization that Magda Gerber founded in California: Resources for Infant Educarers (RIE).

They describe the application of the RIE model in a range of practice settings in the US, the usefulness of the model as a basis for parent education and the way in which the approach is taught. The book concludes by examining the applicability of the RIE approach to the current UK context.

Background

In post-war Hungary, Emmi Pikler developed a model of group care for infants that promoted optimal development and attachment relationships. Pikler's observations of infants and young children began with her experiences as a mother and a family pediatrician. Later, in the large post-war residential institution known as Loczy (see Glossary – renamed the Emmi Pikler National Methodological Institute for Residential Nurseries after her death in 1984), Pikler found ways of caring for infants that avoided institutionalization and promoted optimal development, yet were resource modest. She faced the challenge of how to give individualized care to babies and infants with a limited number of caregivers. From Pikler's appointment as director of the Institute in 1946 until the present day, the Loczy model has been researched (Gerber 1979). Evidence suggests that this approach to group care for infants supports Pikler's claim that the development of the children raised at Loczy in full-time residential care "has been sound, and is similar to the pattern of development of children reared in families" (Pikler 1970, p.92).

Magda Gerber, Pikler's friend and colleague, took the Loczy model of infant care to the US in the 1960s and spent many years working with infants and toddlers, including children with special needs, primarily in the multi-ethnic context of Los Angeles. The model has been promoted and developed for day care and family situations by RIE, a non-profit organization set up by Gerber and dedicated to infants and their caregivers. Although there has been comparatively little research undertaken in the US on this approach, Gerber has, nonetheless, been an influential figure in early childhood debates and education. She has been credited with introducing the concept of "respect" into work with infants and toddlers in the US (Gonzalez-Mena and Widmeyer Eyer 1993). Although the work of Pikler and Gerber is little known in the UK they have influenced infant care not only in the US but in European countries such as Belgium, France and Italy (Penn 1999) and more recently Australia and the Pacific Rim.

The UK context

In the UK, at the present time, early years policies and services are fundamental to government strategies designed to tackle child poverty and long-term social exclusion (Jamieson and Owen 2000). Major government programs such as Sure Start local programs and the National Childcare Strategy (now brought together under the generic term Sure Start) provide resources for statutory and independent sector organizations offering services to young children, families and communities in order to promote and improve their health and well-being and enable parents to work (see Chapter 8 for a more extensive discussion of this).

Gerber's adaptation of the Loczy model as a basis for out-of-family and in-family care for young infants has particular relevance in this context. First, there is no model of infant/caregiver interaction in the UK that is equally applicable to residential, day care, family center or family home settings. Second, in line with the current emphasis on evidence-based practice, the Loczy model is underpinned by substantive research on meeting the developmental and attachment needs of infants and toddlers, although much is still only available in French or Hungarian. Policy-makers need information about alternative child care methods, particularly for children "in need" or "at risk" and for communities with particular social and economic issues and disadvantages. The Loczy model has applicability across social and economic contexts, cultures and settings and particularly for those responsible for developing and implementing family support programs including parenting education. Lastly, although completely child-centered in philosophy, the approach is resource-modest. It is therefore well within the cost-capacity of the smallest day care settings or the poorest families.

In the summer of 2004, a controversy erupted into the British media about a subject which we all thought had been resolved long ago. Does day care harm young children? A long article by Madeline Bunting in *The Guardian* (Bunting 2004) outlined findings from a range of research studies which, she argued, indicated that full-time group care for children under two could lead to anti-social behavior later:

> Research on both sides of the Atlantic has reached remarkably similar conclusions; namely that large quantities of care in a nursery before the age of three increases the incidence of insecurity and aggression in children, and that these damaging effects are still evident years later.

This was picked up by the less moderate press as "Nurseries turning children into thugs" (*London Evening Standard* 8 July 2004) and it was rumored that the government was so concerned about this that it would announce an extension to the period of paid maternity leave.

It had long been accepted by most early years researchers and policy-makers that it is the quality of the day care which matters: poor day care can harm young children but high quality day care is positively beneficial, and indicators of quality have been established on which systems such as registration and inspection are based. A second scandal was highlighted not long after this when a BBC reporter went "under cover" to work in four private day nurseries and filmed cruel and unhygienic practices in three of them.

Again, the press was quick to scare: "Cruelty in the nursery" (*Daily Mail* 12 August 2004). This seemed to re-open the debate about whether or not mothers should be going out to work when their children are young.

It is in this kind of climate, where parents are prey to such scare mongering, that an approach such as RIE can offer some realistic ways forward. The development of "authentic relationships" which are based on deep knowledge of individual children can occur both in the home and in day care settings, preferably both. They nourish attachment, reward parental and caregiver efforts and foster children's individual abilities in ways which allow us to be confident that we have done the best for our children, whatever their circumstances.

RIE principles into practice

In order to understand what is distinctive about the RIE approach to the care and learning of babies it is important to consider its history and development. Emmi Pikler based her theories on principles of child-centered practice that were being developed by pediatricians, psychologists and psychoanalysts in continental Europe in the mid-20th century. Stephanie Petrie describes in her review (Chapter 1) how Pikler developed practice and principles in an integrated way in the Loczy residential nursery in Hungary with children who had been parted from their parents. Magda Gerber then took these principles and developed the RIE model, which is the subject of this book, when she emigrated to the US. As Petrie says: "It is remarkable that the two women continued to collaborate and share ideas at the height of the Cold War when both sides of the Iron Curtain viewed one another with hostility and suspicion." This is only one demonstration of the versatility of this approach which, focused as it is on the unique needs and personalities of individual children, can transcend cultural, social and physical difference and ensure "equal concern" and inclusion for every child. The phrase "equal concern" was used within the Children Act 1989 as a description of care that could ensure equality of treatment for children while still recognising and celebrating their differences: equal but not the same (Children Act 1989 s.XX, cited in Bainham 1990).

We have chosen to describe the basic principles and practices of RIE (Chapter 2) through the words of Magda Gerber herself, writing in *Educaring*, a parents' newsletter in the late 1970s. Her fluent and descriptive writing gives the best possible description of her aim to help parents and carers better understand and support their children from the moment of birth. A quotation from this chapter also appears at the head of each of the other chapters in order to locate all these different examples within the body of her original work and to link the practical implementation back to her basic aims.

But what is a RIE curriculum? If this approach is to be of interest to practitioners in the full range of early years settings, there needs to be a clear enunciation of what it includes in terms of activities and dispositions that promote children's learning. In Chapter 3, Ruth Money outlines what RIE practitioners mean by a curriculum and gives examples of the activities, the planning and the respectful approach to infants that it embodies: "Infants who have been in respectful relationships and have been allowed to play freely do not need to be amused. Such infants have long attention spans for tasks they set for themselves. They are learning to learn."

These descriptions of the basic RIE philosophy and principles are followed by two chapters that outline the ways in which the approach has been used in differing day care settings in the US. In Chapter 4, Catherine Coughlan talks about her family day care (childminding) practice and the way in which she was able to develop it, from inception, to meet RIE principles. She examines and makes us think anew about some issues that we often take for granted, such as mixed age grouping and the extent of children's self-initiated activity: "Facilitating their play was much more important, and productive, than questioning their motives."

Catherine makes a heartfelt plea for improved subsidy for young children's services and this is taken up also by Polly Elam in Chapter 5 as she describes the implementation of the RIE approach in group day care centers. Her challenge to us is to think about how we can provide "excellent" care for babies and what needs to be in place to ensure this. She describes in detail the caregiving routines that underpin the respectful attention given to the children by their carers. She talks about the central role of management and leadership in putting a vision into practice and in working to gather the resources needed for this: "It is not enough to say we are committed, our commitment must be shown through our actions – through the policies we write and strategies, including financial support, which we develop for implementing them."

In Chapter 6 Elizabeth Memel and Lee Fernandez introduce one of the basic elements of RIE's work in the US, the parent–infant classes. The integrated methodology of the organization means that these classes serve as support and development for parents or carers, enriching environments for children and training grounds for RIE practitioners at all levels. The authors describe situations in which all these functions are fulfilled in a number of different environments, including higher education. The joy of their chapter, however, comes as we witness the gradual growth of relaxation and understanding on the part of parents as they come to realize that they can, in

Gerber's words "observe more and do less" and trust themselves to be the experts on their own child. As Memel and Fernandez say in Chapter 6: "The parent then becomes less active and therefore less burdened and frustrated, and the child becomes more active and therefore freer and with fuller access to self-expression."

They also emphasize the importance of a process such as this in empowering and supporting parents as well as their children. This links back to the points made by Stephanie Petrie in Chapter 1 as she considers the usefulness of a time-rich but resource-poor approach such as this for impoverished or vulnerable families: "Intervention must highlight the strengths which families have, rather than underscoring the weaknesses. RIE's non-deficit model features empowerment as a process of change, over time, for parents of young children from any section of society."

Lastly, Stephanie Petrie and Sue Owen look at the potential of the RIE approach for supporting work with babies in the UK. They describe the current situation of both social work and early years services and the drive for integration which the government hopes will transform the way in which services are delivered to children and families in the future. They recognize the firm foundation for child-centered pedagogy that exists in the British educational tradition but also understand some of the current threats to it. They believe that the RIE approach can complement this with a particular and sustainable focus on the care and learning of babies and the support of their parents:

> Welfare services for young children and their families in the UK; from childcare to primary school education, from health services to social housing are implemented within a "market" paradigm. This framework does not always support the individual competencies of young children or their capacity for self-directed learning. Their voices are silent in the "market" and their needs frequently secondary to those of adults, whether service-users or service commissioners or providers.

Interest in early years issues is growing rapidly in the UK and government policy, designed to increase the amount and range of services, has been a major factor in stimulating this interest. The bulk of day care, tightly regulated by government, is provided by the independent sector and regulations include requirements for ongoing staff training and development, infant/toddler curricula and parental involvement. Therefore, we anticipate that the discussions within this volume will directly address some of the most pressing issues in children's services today.

Chapter 1

The Work of Emmi Pikler
and Magda Gerber

Stephanie Petrie

The goal is inner or self-discipline, self-confidence, and joy in the act of cooperation.

Magda Gerber

Emmi Pikler and Magda Gerber

The work of Magda Gerber and her mentor, colleague and friend, Emmi Pikler (1902–1984) has had utility for more than 50 years and in countries with vastly different socio-economic and political systems. Their work began in post-World War Two communist Hungary and Magda Gerber took the principles of respectful care for infants with her with equal effectiveness to the US, the apotheosis of capitalism, in the late 1950s. It is remarkable that the two women continued to collaborate and share ideas at the height of the Cold War when both sides of the Iron Curtain viewed one another with hostility and suspicion (Hobsbawm 1994). Even today, the non-profit organization Resources for Infant Educarers (RIE, pronounced RYE), founded in the US by Magda Gerber to promote respectful care for infants and the Emmi Pikler National Methodological Institute for Residential Nurseries (nicknamed Loczy, after the street in Budapest where the institution is sited) founded by Pikler in 1946 and currently under the directorship of her daughter, Anna Tardos, maintain close links and continue to learn from each other.

Judit Falk (1986), Deputy Director and later Director of Loczy, considered that the main factors influencing the direction of Pikler's work with children was her pediatric training in the 1920s, her experience as a mother and her ten years' experience as a community pediatrician in Budapest before World War Two. Pikler's training in Vienna in the 1920s at the University Children's Hospital under Professors von Pirquet and Salzer was extremely radical in the approach adopted towards young patients. In contrast to child care practices of the day, young children were dressed in clothing that allowed free movement. They were allowed to get out of bed and play if well enough and play corners were set up on the wards. The regime was directed towards cooperative and respectful interaction with children based on observations of their day-to-day behavior. During her studies Pikler also observed that children who were allowed free movement in the home environment sustained fewer accidents because they were physically more practiced and therefore more confident. Her ideas were brought together when her daughter was born in the early 1930s and she experienced at first hand the benefits to child and carer of such a respectful, child-centered approach. During the following decade Emmi Pikler developed her methods with her patients and their families as a community pediatrician and when commissioned by the City of Budapest in 1946 to establish Loczy she was ready to apply her ideas to the care of children deprived of their parental and familial relationships.

Magda Gerber first knew Emmi Pikler as a mother whose child attended the same kindergarten as her own eldest daughter. She describes how she secured Dr. Pikler's services as pediatrician for her children and how greatly she was influenced by her way of relating to them (Gerber and Johnson 1998). Magda Gerber subsequently worked with her mentor at Loczy until she and her family left Hungary for the US in the late 1950s. She found that the family culture of the US in the 1950s and 1960s was not always beneficial to children. However, she also found that the basic principles of respectful care could be used in settings other than residential institutions and were equally effective. She took Pikler's approach and practices into a number of posts she held in those early years: in children's hospitals, schools for autistic children, parenting support programs and, later, day care centers (Gerber and Johnson 1998).

The work of Pikler and Gerber is best known, therefore, in Hungary and the US, although child care provision in some European countries, particularly Italy, Belgium and France, has also been influenced. Emmi Pikler's reputation with some European child care specialists is especially high: "Cocever...argues that Emmi Pikler, the director of the Loczy Institute deserves a similar status to the other great early childhood educators such as Maria Montessori and Celestin Freinet" (Penn 1999, p.28).

It has been suggested, however, that one reason why Pikler's work has had less influence in Europe than other child development theorists and practitioners such as Montessori, was that initially some children placed at Loczy were the children of dissidents – removed from their families for political reasons (Penn 1999). Since the reason for the out-of-family care was unacceptable to many people, the quality of the care was overlooked. Nevertheless, since her death in 1984, Pikler's work has steadily become more influential in many countries:

> The work on motor development and the ideas about the learning process have interested those who work with children with "special needs". Parents groups have been set up, offering them the "Pikler" approach to bringing up their children. More recently, with the analysis of differences between the "maternal relationship" and the "professional relationship", we are seeing foster carers and family day carers drawing on this experience. The most recent development is the interest shown by researchers and academics in the rich material provided by observations and their analysis. These contribute to new advances in understanding early development and conditions for improving development. (Appell 2003)

In the UK, the work of these women is less well-known. This may be because public policy and private attitudes towards education and care of young children are somewhat different from those of our European neighbors. Unlike most of Europe, such services in the UK are provided as a necessary aid for working parents or those with parenting problems rather than as valuable services for children (Burden, Cooper and Petrie 2000; Novak et al. 1997; Statham, Dillon and Moss 2001).

This chapter will summarize research evidence about outcomes for children resulting from poor early care and highlight the importance of attachment theory, both influential on Pikler's work. A review of the key elements of her approach to care for children under three years old in residential institutions, and that of Magda Gerber with parents and in out-of-family care in the community will be outlined and evidence for effectiveness examined. The chapter will end with comments about the relevance of their work for young children and their carers in the UK today, an aspect which will be discussed in greater detail in the last chapter. The terms "carer" and "parent" will be used interchangeably to reflect the wide variety in family forms in the UK today.

Outcomes for children resulting from poor early care

The detrimental effects of residential care on very young children and the impact of "maternal deprivation" in infancy on an individual's mental health in adulthood became widely known at about the same time Emmi Pikler became director of Loczy in 1946. Researchers such as Spitz (1945) and Bowlby (1951) demonstrated the impact of poor early care on health, growth and development from infancy through to adulthood. Spitz showed that institutional care for infants and young children led to low resistance to disease, high mortality rates, impaired motor and cognitive development and emotional incapacity. Bowlby's observations of children separated from their parents in wartime, as orphans, evacuees or refugees and the early experiences of young people involved in crime, led him to develop attachment theory, drawing on many other disciplines. Without a positive attachment relationship in early years, Bowlby argued, an individual's capacity to forge satisfactory relationships and achieve good mental health in adulthood would be impaired: "[T]he prolonged deprivation of the young child of maternal care may have grave and far-reaching effects in his character and so on the whole of his future life" (Bowlby 1951, cited in Clarke and Clarke 2000, p.13).

Attachment theory has been the most significant theoretical contribution this century to our understanding of the psychological development of children. Attachment can be defined as "the constellation of feelings and behaviours demonstrated by babies towards their parents and other caregivers" (Sutton 1994, p.41). Bowlby's monograph (1951) focused on mother/child separation and he argued that if a child was deprived of "good mothering" for the first two and a half years of life, the damaging effects on the growing child were unlikely to be mitigated, with likely adverse effects in adulthood. Bowlby's initial hypothesis was critiqued on a number of grounds, including sampling bias in his initial empirical study (Clarke and Clarke 2000). Feminists and others argued that his assumption that the primary carer was female excluded the influence of fathers or male partners and placed the sole blame for adverse outcomes for children on mothers (Riley 1983). This over-simplification of attachment theory was used to justify social policies aimed at women in the 1950s and 1960s in the UK to prevent them entering the labor market, on the grounds that this was bad for children (Williams 1995). In fact, the reasons were economic and as labor market and social factors have changed again, so has social policy towards working mothers of small children. In the UK, as in the US, poor women are now encouraged to enter the workforce as a way out of poverty for themselves and their children. As discussed in the last chapter, child care policies often focus on the needs of adults and the wider society to the detriment of children.

Bowlby continued researching and theorizing until his death in 1990 and other empiricists and theorists (Ainsworth *et al.* 1978; Clarke and Clarke 1976; Parkes, Stevenson-Hinde and Marris 1991; Rutter 1981) have added to our understanding. Attachment behaviors of babies towards their primary carers and carers' responses towards them, and the implications for children, are better understood and underpin much of today's child care policy and practice in the UK. For example, the *Framework for the Assessment of Children in Need and their Families* (DoH, DfEE, HO 2000), the mandatory policy and associated guidance for assessing vulnerable children, is based on attachment theory within an eco-systemic framework and reflects current research evidence and practice wisdom (Sidebotham 2001). In other words, the causality of child harm is complex, and any assessment must be child-centered and take account of attachment relationships, positives as well as deficits, and potential for improvements:

> What has stood the test of time has been the proposition that the qualities of parent-child relationships constitute a central aspect of parenting, that the development of social relationships occupies a crucial role in personality growth, and that abnormalities in relationships are important in many types of psychopathology. (Rutter, M., cited in Howe *et al.* 1999, p.10)

The key elements of Bowlby's theory remain useful and are:

- The attachment figure – the individual, usually the primary caregiver, with whom the child seeks to maintain contact and who provides a strong, all encompassing and consistent feeling of security.

- Attachment behavior – that is, behavior manifested by the child in order to maintain or obtain closeness to the attachment figure. This includes *proximity-seeking*, the *secure-base effect* and *separation protest*. These behaviors occur most readily between about six or seven months of age and three years. (See the "strange situation" test developed by Mary Ainsworth [Ainsworth *et al.* 1978].)

- Caregiving behaviors – are the responses by the primary carer to the attachment behavior of the child directed towards soothing, comforting and understanding; e.g. sensitivity, acceptance, and accessibility (emotional as well as physical).

- Separation behaviors – *protest, withdrawal* and *detachment* are the emotional behaviors children display when separated from their attachment figure and are similar to the emotional stages of bereavement shown by adults (Fahlberg 1994; Parkes *et al.* 1991).

- Attachment classification system – the classic paradigm proposed by Bowlby's colleague Mary Ainsworth (Ainsworth *et al.* 1978) and later enhanced by Main and Soloman (1986), classifies attachment relationships into *Insecure and Avoidant, Secure, Insecure and Ambivalent or Resistant, Insecure and Disorganized* and *Non-attachments.* (These classifications are observable in all societies and their proportions appear to correlate with the overall cultural characteristics of the society, e.g. whether the social emphasis is on competition or cooperation.)

The importance of play and self-directed learning as experiences necessary for a young child's optimal growth and development across all dimensions – physical, intellectual and emotional – was highlighted by other important child development theorists at this time. Jean Piaget (1975) viewed children as active participants from birth in the process of knowledge acquisition. He argued that children pass through stages of cognitive development, each characterized by particular modes of thought. A child's physical activity from its earliest days, according to Piaget, leads to cognitive activity, and the development of coping skills and self-esteem. Erik Erikson (1950) emphasized the importance of trust developed through relationships with others, alongside autonomy, as critical to a child's optimal development.

Since the 1940s and 1950s these and other child development theorists have continued to explore the world of the child and extend our understanding of the essential conditions necessary for optimal development. What is remarkable, however, is that at the same time as Bowlby, Piaget and Erikson were developing their highly influential theories, Emmi Pikler was also exploring the same issues but from the standpoint of a participant and carer as well as a researcher and theorist.

Emmi Pikler and Loczy

Essentially a pragmatist, Pikler took the view that while there were children to be cared for they were her first priority. However, she was also a scientist trained in the positivist tradition and from the beginning of her directorship of Loczy, although resources were scarce, she established a rigorous system for evaluating effectiveness and a scientific inquiry into gross motor development in infants (David and Appell 2001). According to her colleague, Judit Falk (1986), Emmi Pikler had three main goals. First, to care for infants and young children in a way that promoted optimal development and attachment relationships of a special kind. Second, she wanted to evaluate the care regime to determine whether positive outcomes for children could be achieved in an institution. And last, she wished to pursue the scientific study of gross motor development and its significance in infants and small children. Pikler began with 35 children under three years old and quickly found that professionally trained carers, known as "nurses", did not have the understanding or motivation to adopt the practices she saw as critical for the well-being of the children. Her co-worker and head caregiver, Maria Reinitz, noted their concerns:

> They do not really care for the children: they wash them down, clean them up, see that they get food, etc. – if possible in a matter of minutes and with the least possible exertion. Whenever they can they let some other person do these things. They mainly care for the linens and so much time is given to taking custody, distributing, incessantly counting and registering linens, that there is no time left for children. (Falk 1986, p.40)

Pikler and Reinitz dismissed the professionally trained "nurses" within three months and employed instead young women from rural areas with little education but an interest in children. They were asked to make a three-year commitment and be prepared to establish a close relationship with their charges (Falk 1979). The young women were trained in the Pikler approach and quickly became sufficiently familiar with the regime to be able to be spontaneous and engage with the children. It's worth noting that choosing, training, and supervising carers still remains a critical issue in out-of-family care, and in relation to RIE-based day care is discussed more fully in Chapter 7. David and Appell (2001) in their study of Loczy in 1971 commented that the staffing approach developed by Pikler continued to be effective: "It seems as if, with increasing experience and a true grasp of the prescribed attitudes, the nurses are able to assimilate them, make them their own, and spontaneously apply them" (p.119).

The Loczy regime was built on four main principles underpinning care for children (see Chapter 2; David and Appell 2001):

- The importance of independent activity.

- The importance of a privileged relationship with a caring adult.

- The importance of an environment that fosters the child's awareness of her/himself and others.

- The importance of good physical health as a basis for the other three elements.

These basic principles underpin much of the RIE approach today (Gerber 1997; Gerber 1998; Gerber and Johnson 1998) and will be described in the following chapters. At Loczy, these principles were manifested in a care regime that involved a number of inviolable conditions. A framework was established within which each child's individual needs, for an authentic primary relationship and autonomy through which to learn and develop, were met. This framework had to take account of the poor resources available that meant many children had to be cared for by few adults in surroundings that were very basic. Children of roughly the same developmental stage were placed in groups. Pikler observed that clustering toddlers and babies together is satisfactory for neither group as their physical and emotional needs are not compatible. This is discussed more fully in Chapter 3. Furthermore, she observed that even young infants notice and touch one another. In fact, they learn to be social and cooperative naturally from their earliest days (Gerber 1979). This level of cooperation and minimal conflict was observed by David and Appell in 1971 during their study of Loczy, and is discussed more fully below.

The children's groups at Loczy were large, initially ten later eight, with three caregivers to each group. Three staff covered the 24 hour period between them, although there was permanent cover for holidays or sickness. Continuity of care was achieved in three ways. First, all basic care tasks were carried out in a uniform and prescribed way and were a response to close observation of the individual child. Such elements as voice tone, eye contact, lack of hurry and information to the child about the task in hand gave even the smallest infant the opportunity to participate, help or protest. In other words, the children were able to be subjects not objects in activities affecting them, to have as much choice as possible and were allowed to express themselves even when an adult agenda had to be paramount. As will be explored later in this book, the Pikler/Gerber method of care involves even the smallest infants by explaining in advance what the adult is intending to do, waiting for some small response from the infant and talking to the infant about what the adult notices about them, for example, he has a wet nappy and seems uncomfortable. The second way of achieving continuity was through the daily observations of each child recorded by the caregiver on duty for the oncoming carer. Very quickly carers were able to observe and note the smallest developmental achievements rather than merely listing what the child ate or drank. Consequently the oncoming carer was fully attuned to the contemporary world of each child. Finally, each child was able to experience total and consistent attention during the intimate caring activities of bathing and nappy-changing because staff turnover was minimal, the "key worker" approach was consistent, and the environment permitted children maximum freedom to develop physical and social skills without interference. The children, confident and relaxed, were able to cooperate with each other and their carers. They were not needy children, competing with each other for their carer's attention, behavior that can place great strain on responsible adults:

> A nurse can devote herself fully to the child she is taking care of at any one moment – giving time, attention and interest that is needed – only if she can be sure that the other children are in good spirits and busy following their individual interests. She needs to know that none are crying from neglect or in need of help as they wait for their turn, but are all moving around playing, trying out their abilities, exploring their surroundings, changing positions, "handling" things and getting along with other children. (Falk 1986, p.42)

Loczy provided an environment for children that fostered their independence yet provided close, loving relationships. These two factors, a safe environment that supports self-initiated activity and the way in which the child is treated in care situations, are fundamental to the work of Emmi Pikler in residential care and, as will be described later, Magda Gerber in her work with parents and day care providers.

Magda Gerber

Madga Gerber, as she explains later in this book, first met Emmi Pikler in Budapest when she consulted her about her young daughter who was unwell. She was so impressed by Dr. Pikler's respectful care of her daughter that she later worked at Loczy and studied there. After the 1956 revolution in Hungary, Gerber came to the US with her husband and children. The family settled permanently in Los Angeles, after a year on the east coast. For some years, Gerber worked as a child therapist, first in a children's hospital and later with autistic children at the Dubnoff School in North Hollywood. In 1968 she developed and directed the Pilot Infant Program at the school, where she took the basic philosophy of Loczy and began to apply it to her work with parents. In all her work, Magda Gerber integrated children with special needs and from widely differing cultures and backgrounds (Gerber and Johnson 1998). She already found the difference in cultures quite marked: "I have felt sometimes like the bridge between Dr. Pikler and

American society. The lifestyle in this country makes it very difficult to raise a baby the way Emmi wanted" (Gerber 1998, p.189).

Her reputation as a practitioner spread and in 1972 Tom Forrest, a pediatrician and Clinical Assistant Professor of Pediatrics at Stanford University, invited Gerber to become co-director of a new project, the Demonstration Infant Program (DIP). DIP was commissioned by the Children's Health Council in Palo Alto, California as part of a preventive mental health strategy. The goal of the program was to "mainstream" high-risk children with children without additional or special needs. Through the DIP program, Gerber was able to work out a way of helping parents/carers observe their own children, so as to better understand their cues. She also modeled respectful interaction with infants without disempowering or de-skilling their carers. She and Forrest worked with groups of four or five babies and their parents for two hours once a week. The DIP program included babies from five months old to two years old, but they were placed in groups of similar developmental stage, as at Loczy. The environment was also modeled on Loczy, allowing maximum freedom of movement in safety with minimal distraction from a child's own self-initiated activity. Gerber or Forrest remained with the babies and the parents observed from another room with the other demonstrator. Selective intervention was modeled.

"Dr. Forrest and I modeled "selective intervention" showing *when* and *how* to intervene in the children's play by remaining available without being intrusive. The demonstrator would intervene if the child's safety was involved, or if the child was too frightened or frustrated in solving a problem. The goal was to encourage the children to participate in the solution. The DIP staff held the belief that non-intervention, or non-interruption of play helps children develop competence in problem-solving skills. This, in turn, requires trust on the part of the parent or carer. We believed that children are very good problem-solvers if given the opportunity" (Gerber and Johnson 1998, p.17).

Their work was based on observation of the infant and feedback to the infant and carers, combined with recognizing the importance of self-directed gross motor movement. In many ways, Gerber was taking the same approach in the DIP program with parents that Pikler took with the Loczy staff. That is, helping adults acquire the knowledge and skill to work out the needs of their individual baby through an interactive relationship. This is rather different from teaching adults how to care for the generic baby. Clearly, there is commonality between infants and children at similar developmental stages, but to Pikler and Gerber the relationship between the adult and child, with the child as an active participant, is critical to determining and meeting the individual needs of each unique baby. Treating children with respect means acknowledging they have a right to information given in an appropriate way and a right to autonomy, as well as consistent, loving care. This does not mean, however, abdicating responsibility as an adult. Children cannot always follow their own inclinations, and directive intervention is needed. "Authenticity" (see Glossary) means the adult must accept the responsibility of authority and be honest about it, while allowing the child to express anger or be upset. The DIP model of parenting classes was incorporated into RIE parenting programs and will be discussed in Chapter 6.

The work of Forrest and Gerber influenced out-of-family care in a range of settings in California through their involvement in state training programs and the subsequent activities of students such as Janet Gonzalez-Mena (Gonzalez-Mena and Widmeyer Eyer 1993). In order to promote the philosophy of respectful interaction with infants more proactively, they established Resources for Infant Educarers (RIE) in 1978, a year after the ending of the DIP program.

The non-profit organization, RIE, was established to offer training to those working with infants in out-of-family care and guidance classes for parents. The philosophy and methods are derived from Emmi Pikler's work at Loczy, but adapted for parents and carers in the complex, "poverty amongst plenty," multicultural society of the US (Gerber 1979; Gerber 1997). Subsequent chapters written by RIE practitioners in the US demonstrate how this philosophy and methods are applied in a range of out-of-family day care settings and with parents. However, although the work of Pikler and Gerber has been long-lasting, what evidence is there for the effectiveness of Loczy and RIE?

Evidence of effectiveness

Loczy

Emmi Pikler was a pediatrician and trained in the positivist tradition of scientific research. From when she became the first director at Loczy in 1946, comprehensive records of the development of all children were kept, primarily to assist carers meet the needs of children, but also providing a rich source of data.

> Dr. Pikler's project makes it clear that the proper operation of a center for children requires means of another order altogether, as elaborate and complex as for the operation of a hospital. Luxurious rooms and costly materials can be dispensed with, but not scrupulously established clinical

files, recorded observations, a group reflection on institutional functioning, and a commitment to research (David and Appell 2001, p.114)

Pikler and her colleagues and subsequent directors of Loczy wrote and presented papers at conferences in Hungary and elsewhere; a comprehensive
list of these can be obtained from Loczy (see Glossary). Most of these,
written in Hungarian or French, have been inaccessible to those working in
English-speaking countries, although a few have been translated. One of
these, funded by the World Health Organization, is an interesting follow-up
study of young people and adults raised as infants in Loczy (Falk and Pikler
1988). The study has some methodological weaknesses, for example, there
was no control group against which to compare outcomes. The definition of
educational achievement, one of the measures of optimal development, was
linked to school performance and it is impossible to know if the standard
was the same throughout Hungary or how Hungarian schools compared
with other countries. No qualitative data was collected from either the
children who grew up in Loczy or the family adults who subsequently lived
with them, so their experiences and perceptions are unknown. However,
there is sufficient data to suggest that most of the children were living in
families and communities in a way that was comparable to children who had
remained with their birth family. As discussed later, this is a most
uncommon outcome for children who have spent their early lives in
institutional care.

Myriam David and Genevieve Appell, much respected for their extensive research with neglected and deprived children and out-of-family care,
visited Loczy in 1971 to undertake a short but systematic observation of the
care approaches and children (David and Appell 2001). Their only reserva-
tion was that within most families the level of conflict is greater than that
experienced day-to-day by children at Loczy. David and Appell wondered if
the children, therefore, were fully prepared for the cut and thrust of family
life. Nevertheless, their conclusions were that the Loczy children achieved
optimal development and established healthy attachment relationships:

> In conclusion we would like to stress the value of the institutional model
> created at Loczy, the preceding reservations not withstanding. It succeeds
> in preserving the children from serious neglect, guarantees them sound
> development, a structuring of their psyche, as well as capacities for sound
> relationships.

Such results are rarely achieved because they require that the following
two obstacles commonly found in institutions be overcome:

- On the one hand, the reluctance, if not refusal, at all levels of responsibility to give priority to the needs of the child...

- On the other hand, a difficulty in accepting the fact that the care of children raised in institutions during their first years requires special competence, and therefore training and supervision; being a woman with heartfelt motivation, maternal instinct, spontaneity or just plain common sense is not enough.

(David and Appell 2001, p.146)

Finally, film of the children's gross motor development and behavior formed an early part of record-keeping at Loczy and continues to this day (see Glossary). These films and videos allow the viewer to observe the minutiae of gross and fine motor development and interaction between adult and child at key moments such as bathing or feeding, and show clearly the approach developed by Pikler.

In summary, although much of the academic work of Pikler and her colleagues has not been translated into English, there is a body of evidence, including observations of the children themselves over many decades, that is accessible to those in the UK without command of French or Hungarian. It is evident that Emmi Pikler did create an environment in a large institution where very young children thrived and achieved their potential. For practitioners in the UK, this is almost unbelievable in view of the overwhelming evidence that has shown that such conditions are usually psychologically and developmentally harmful. Following the work of Bowlby (1973, 1979, 1980, 1988), Mary Ainsworth *et al.* (1978), the filmed observations undertaken in the 1960s and 1970s by James and Joyce Robertson (see Glossary), Michael Rutter (1975) and others, policy and practice in the UK in the 1970s and 1980s moved away from placing small children in institutions. Substitute family care, fostering or adoption, has been the practice norm for three decades. However, there is increasing evidence to show that substitute family care, unless it is the early adoption of healthy infants, has a high rate of placement breakdown, with damaging consequences for children, especially their ability to form healthy attachment relationships:

All the major research studies have confirmed that long-term foster care placements are particularly vulnerable to breakdown. Despite making plans for children to remain on a long-term basis in a foster home, they are often moved or they live with uncertainty hanging over their future placement. This has led to serious questioning of the foster care system and concerns about the child's experience of foster care. (Rushton 2003, p.18)

Later studies have confirmed that it is the quality of the relationship between the child and their primary carer that determines the stability of the placement (Wilson, Petrie and Sinclair 2003). Since repeated placement breakdown is now a feature of substitute family care in the UK (Rushton 2003), it is perhaps timely to consider Pikler's work in relation to preparing and supporting young children and their carers before, during and after out-of-family placements. A common, child-centered care approach would go some way to providing children with the consistency and security they need to thrive. Pikler has demonstrated how to establish an environment and care regime responsive to the needs of young children that promotes optimal development and healthy attachments.

RIE

In the US, little consistent research has been undertaken, however, the influence of Magda Gerber as a practitioner and pedagogue, mentioned earlier, is an indication her ideas and methods have been found effective in many settings. Her practical approach to group care is embedded in the tradition of respect for children's competency shared by most major theorists such as Piaget (1975) and Erikson (1950) and pre-school education programs such as the world renowned Reggio Emilia (Reggio Children 1996). As discussed earlier, the emphasis on the importance of unfettered gross motor development in the development of an infant's cognitive abilities is well researched, as are attachment behaviors and disorders. More recently, evidence is emerging confirming young babies are not passive beings but are very sophisticated processors of experiences that provide the knowledge and skills needed to develop (BBC 2002; Gopnik, Meltzoff and Kuhl 1999). Other research has confirmed the benefits to children of lying on their backs (FSID 2004) and being allowed unfettered gross motor development (BBC 2002b). If the key elements of respectful care for infants in groups developed by Pikler and Gerber are considered alongside many significant research findings on aspects of child development, then the value of their work is easily seen. The significant characteristic of Pikler and Gerber as child care theorists and practitioners has been the integrated nature of their work. Observing, thinking, caring for children and teaching were not separate activities to them but part of a unified approach. They had to find better ways to care for children because the children were there to be cared for; they could not wait.

An approach that can promote optimal development and secure attachment relationships and has proven benefits is important. However, Pikler and Gerber have also developed a method that can be adapted for different cultures and countries, for use in many different settings: home, day care, residential care, and in settings that have minimal resources. It would seem, however, that further research of outcomes for children, at Loczy and of RIE in the US is now needed.

Relevance of the work of Pikler and Gerber to young children and their carers in the UK

Poverty among families with young children increased significantly in the UK from the beginning of the Thatcher government in 1979 (Burden, Cooper and Petrie 2000). Since the first New Labour government was elected in 1997, economic and social policies have promoted paid work as the way out of poverty, recast as "social exclusion" for poor families, particularly lone mothers (Burden *et al.* 2000). Inevitably, this means children need day care. As a result providing day care subsidies for parents and increasing the availability, accessibility and quality of day care for children is another government priority and will be discussed more fully in the last chapter.

Day care in the UK is expensive for the individual family relative to the same services in other European countries. Also, in many other countries day care is seen as a collective responsibility and subsidized via much higher levels of taxation. However, in the UK, if parents are not poor enough to be entitled to government subsidy, the only other way to access state-funded day care would be if their child was assessed as being a "child in need" – the legal passport to state-funded family support services (Children Act 1989, s.17, cited in Bainham 1990). Recent studies have shown that in these circumstances, places are usually allocated to meet adult need and, as soon as family circumstances improve, funding is withdrawn (Novak *et al.* 1997; Statham *et al.* 2001). Should family circumstances deteriorate and the adults assessed as needing relief once more from parenting, it is unlikely the child would return to the same day care provider – retainers are rarely paid to keep places open. The child, therefore, receives a service that is episodic and inconsistent. Even when parents receive state subsidies to purchase day care for their children, quality is often variable and choice limited, a situation that is particularly difficult for parents working unsocial hours (Craig *et al.* 1999). Pre-school education is provided by the state for all three and four-year-old children whose parents want this, but these part-time places are usually within a school. Concerns have been expressed that drawing young children into a formalized school setting risks undermining their own learning and development pathways. How young children learn is well-known, as outlined earlier, and this can be hampered by formal curriculum approaches which do not emphasize the individual needs of each child (BBC 2003, 2004; Pugh 1996). The recent development of the Foundation Stage, running from three to six years of age, its adoption as part of the National Curriculum, and an observation-based assessment profile for this age group, have all gone a long way to alleviating these fears (DfES 2000). However, early years specialists are concerned over inappropriate aspects of the formal curriculum that can still affect provision. The Government's announcement in April 2004 of a pilot project to provide part-time nursery education for two-year-olds has fueled concerns of this kind, and make it even more urgent to consider effective approaches to provision for the youngest children.

Emmi Pikler and Magda Gerber, building on many years of child observation, looked for ways in which the full potential of every unique child, in whatever setting, could be brought to fruition. There is some evidence to suggest the Loczy/RIE infants have less stressful interactions with others. In other words, they are at peace with themselves and therefore are easier to care for. Feeding, sleeping, and behavioral problems are minimal and short-lived. In complex societies that are comparatively affluent, there are still many parents of babies and infants who have to enter the workforce for economic reasons and place their children in day care. A method that can be used by parents and day care providers to look after small children in a way that is complementary, builds strong relationships between adults and children and supports a child's optimal development must surely benefit both carers and their children.

Summary and conclusion

The key elements of the work of Piker and Gerber rest on understanding that young children are interdependent (see Chapter 3) with adults, needing appropriate but participative care, yet also needing to be independent at times. Children need loving, interactive relationships and practical care such as food and shelter, and so on. However, they also need independence so they can learn what their bodies can do and, by exploring their world with confidence, develop their cognitive, emotional and social capacities. This is so in all settings where young children are cared for, including their families of origin, and is necessary for any child in order to achieve optimal development and healthy attachments.

Through her action research, Emmi Pikler was able to promote optimal development and healthy attachments for young children in an institutional environment when, as discussed earlier, many studies had shown institutional care to be highly damaging to young children. Magda Gerber was able to adapt these insights to benefit children living with their birth families in communities in the very different circumstances faced in complex, Western societies. Societies such as the US and the UK are characterized by a polarization of extreme wealth and extreme poverty (Jones and Novak 1999) and the well-being of children can become secondary as parents try to meet the economic and social demands made of them. In these societies too, there is little collective responsibility for children, who are seen to be the sole responsibility of their parents or parent. As mentioned above, when parents of young children are expected to enter the workforce, similar ways of providing consistent, quality care in home and day care settings could do much to relieve infant distress and parental anxiety.

However, the most important characteristic of the work of Pikler and Gerber is that they have demonstrated an effective way of bringing up *all* children, not just those separated from their parents for short or long periods. This method can be adopted with equal benefit by any parent in their own home, as Magda Gerber explains in the next chapter.

Chapter 2

RIE Principles and Practices

Magda Gerber

Introduction by the editors

In the winter of 1979, Magda Gerber and her associates within Resources for Infant Educarers (RIE) in California began the publication of a newsletter called *Educaring*, designed to keep in touch with those who had shown an interest in the RIE approach to caring for babies. Her contributions to the newsletter form one of the only collections we have of her own writing and, as such, we have used them in order to create a chapter that introduces the basic principles and practices of RIE. These will be expanded upon and shown within different contexts in the chapters which follow, but here we have the background and the basic approach of RIE in Magda's own words.

Figure 2.1 Magda Gerber

The influence of Emmi Pikler and Loczy

Historically, I was the same bewildered mother as many of you, although at a different time (decades ago) and in a different place (Hungary). When I met Dr. Emmi Pikler, her ideas seemed so natural, sensible and simple that I tried to learn more about them. Dr. Pikler developed her unusual approach to caring for infants during the ten years she practiced as a private pediatrician in Budapest, Hungary. In 1946 she applied the same philosophy to infants without families raised at the National Methodological Institute for Residential Nurseries (Loczy) in Budapest (see Glossary). Her talents as a scientific investigator and a practitioner involved in the minutest details of the everyday care of infants make her sound approach both practical and believable.

I first met Emmi Pikler when my children were five and two years old. I often tell the story of my first child who says, "I brought Emmi into your life. Therefore I launched your career." It's true, because Emmi's daughter, Anna, who is a psychologist at Loczy (Anna Tardos is currently Director of the Loczy Institute) and my daughter went to kindergarten together. So when our doctor was not available my daughter said, "Why don't you call Anna's mommy who is a pediatrician?" Of course, I knew about Anna's mommy, because everyone in Budapest who had a young child knew about Emmi Pikler. She had been an extremely controversial figure in Hungary. There were almost two camps. One for whom Emmi was the prophet and whatever she said they would do almost blindly, and another who absolutely hated her. Many professional pediatricians couldn't believe that a person really truly would want to visit a family every week, which she did. Every week. And then she'd spend hours just watching the children. If you had a child who was constantly sick, she came constantly. Of course, a Pikler baby wasn't constantly sick. Everybody would say that right away. The joke was that if a child was sick, she had to call a consultant because she had "unlearned" to be with sick children. She had only been with healthy children. Now the fact is that if you do lots of good preventive, healthy things, such as ensuring the child has good nutrition, good care, good everything, they are rarely sick.

What Emmi Pikler liked to do best was discuss everything with a pregnant woman. She would explain what she stood for. If it didn't work, she would stop. And she stopped with many families, very gently and with no animosity. She just said, "Look, you thought that you agreed with me and I can see that you don't. It's hard on you. It's fine. There are many other ways to raise children. Go ahead, but I'm wasting my time." She was an original. Which means she cannot be compared to anybody else. She had her own ideas. Her own way of carrying them out. She was a very complex person who had an enormous impact on people. She didn't like to just give advice without knowing a lot about the child, the mother, the situation. When she said something it came out very sincerely – a very strong message, even though she didn't deliver it in a strong style.

RIE principles

Since my days with Dr. Pikler in Hungary, I have applied her philosophy to my work with infants in California. Emmi Pikler found it most difficult when people picked up some of the philosophy, but not the essence. Many people absorbed some of it, but they didn't quite understand the underlying principles. Similarly, I now go to places and can see immediately if people understand the spirit of the approach even if they do things differently from the way I would. Or, on the other hand, they do things almost as an imitation of what they have seen me do and yet they have no idea why they are doing it. Our organization, Resources for Infant Educarers (RIE) grew out of encouragement we received from parents and professionals who successfully used our philosophy and urged us to offer training to infant carers. The RIE approach aims to achieve a balance between adult stimulation and independent exploration by the infant.

Respect

Respect is the basis of the RIE philosophy. We not only respect babies, we demonstrate our respect every time we interact with them. Respecting a child means treating even the youngest infant as a unique human being, not as an object. Nobody knows exactly when an infant begins to understand language. But infants do begin to pay attention to the world around them slowly and gradually from birth onward. To talk to your baby from the first hour of her life is not only pleasant and soothing to the baby, it is a relief for the parent to say how she or he feels and what he or she wants. It is also the beginning of a lifetime of communication.

A basic principle is to respect and trust a baby's inborn capacities. His natural desire to learn and take in from the world is very important. And anything that intrudes upon that disturbs the natural flow. Our role is to create an environment in which the child can best do all the things that the child would do naturally. The misleading thing about this is that it sounds so easy. Most parents would say, "Sure, that's what I want. Of course, that's what I want." If you follow that now in this country (US), it's fully against what the whole society is all about. The whole society pushes you constantly. In education, what was expected at age seven in second grade is now done in nursery school, but what Emmi Pikler really stood for seems, in contrast, the simplest, the most natural thing to do. She didn't say work more. She said work less. Enjoy more. Work less. Just sit and enjoy your child. It's a miracle. It does happen in front of your eyes. Yes, of course you have to be sensitive to your child's needs. The child has to feel your caring presence. But you don't have to teach. You don't have to buy more gadgets. You don't have to do anything. Both of you can just exist and enjoy the developing relationship between you. Doesn't that sound simpler and easier? But it isn't, because each of us is bombarded to buy books and follow everyone who tells us what to do. Now, if that's what you hear, it's hard to resist. What if you just wait and your child won't do it? How can you really trust?

In many cultures, people have been led to think that unless infants are taught, they don't learn. In the guise of teaching has come tight swaddling, being tied to boards, being carried in slings and pouches, placed in infant seats, jumpers or walkers, being immobilized as well as exercised. You believe the person who tells you how marvellous it is when you have a bouncer. While the child is bouncing, you can take your shower and you can even be on the phone. The child is safe and doesn't fall down, and is happy and doesn't cry. Everybody in his or her right mind would feel that it's not a natural thing for a child to hang there and bounce. And yet it's so easy to believe it. The lifestyle in the US makes it very difficult to raise a baby the way Emmi Pikler wanted. She had a strong feeling that if you give a young child a peaceful beginning where the basic idea is that the child develops a natural rhythm, a rhythm of life which becomes predictable for both the baby and the parent, who can then say, for example, "I know my child sleeps from this time to this time and then I can get my work done." It really doesn't include lots of driving children from place to place, expecting children to behave and live as an appendage of an adult, since then the child cannot behave according to her own needs. She has to adapt to the needs of the parents. And so, first we have to let the child develop his own rhythm and then later he can grow more into adult life. This is the time when you want to let go. You want to feel at ease, soft. Not hurried. Not pushed. Not wanting to achieve. Very few things are done with the thought, "How will what I do now affect my child one year, ten years, twenty-five years from now?" And this is what Emmi Pikler meant for us to keep in mind. Where are you really going? What is your real goal?

Autonomy

Gross motor development happens naturally when an infant has plenty of space to move in a safe, age-appropriate and challenging environment. Nowadays, people find it hard to believe that this uninterrupted absorption is learning. However, if you watch babies who are allowed to move freely and without interference you will see that they learn to move gracefully and securely and, through endless repetition and practice, they become well balanced (see Figure 2.2). These kinds of sensory experiences are learning, and are a great pleasure for a parent to watch! A father who once asked me whether he should exercise his baby or take him to a gym class was intrigued when I suggested that he imitate all his baby's movements for about one hour and decide then if his baby needed an additional workout.

Figure 2.2 Without interference most children learn to move gracefully and securely

We have a basic trust in the infant to be an initiator, an explorer eager to learn what he is ready for. We provide an environment for the infant that is physically safe, cognitively challenging, and emotionally nurturing. We give her plenty of time for uninterrupted play. We do not teach her how to move or how to play, but rather observe her carefully to understand her communications and her needs. During care activities – diapering (nappy-changing), feeding, bathing, dressing, and so on – we encourage even the tiniest infant to become an active participant rather than a passive recipient of the activities.

The new baby at home

The appropriate place for your baby is his own room. He should be within hearing distance, but away from too much activity. Theories and fads keep changing, from advising you to sleep together in the "family bed", to putting the infant far enough away not to be disturbed by his crying. Some experts tell you to take your baby with you wherever you go, to give her security. We believe that babies derive security from both being near their parents and also being allowed to freely explore their environment on their own.

Buy a basket or small crib, a diapering table, a chest of drawers, a small plastic bathtub and an approved car safety seat. What you do not need are jolly jumpers, swings, walkers and high chairs. For the first two months, babies' most valuable play objects, and even mobiles, are their own hands, their parents' faces, the bars of their cribs, their blankets, and so on. The first "toy" we recommend is a cotton or linen (never silk) square, about 20"×20", hemmed and pulled up into a peak, to be visible to an infant lying on her back.

Regularity and predictability help babies develop their inner rhythm of sleeping, eating and alertness. It is best if a baby can spend the first six to eight weeks rather undisturbed in her own environment, and parents give themselves time without extra activities. It is exhausting to live with a new baby; parents would do well to take it easy and give themselves rest rather than more activities. The way you begin life with your newborn will set a pattern, a kind of blueprint for future relationships.

All of us experience self-confidence under some circumstances and fear and doubt under others. Security comes from believing either that I can handle the situation I am in (self-trust) or that in some way the situation will be taken care of (trust in the environment). Infancy is a time of great dependence. Nevertheless babies should be allowed to do things for themselves from the very beginning. Here are some examples:

- Mother places her nipple on baby's cheek. The rooting reflex moves baby's head towards the breast.

- Father looks at baby with outstretched arms and asks: "Do you want to be picked up?" Baby is given time to make a choice.

- A five-month-old boy reaches for a doll. He wriggles his body closer to it and finally is able to reach it.

- An eleven-month-old's ball gets stuck under a shelf. Her expression shows anger. She kicks her legs. Parent says, "Oh, your ball got stuck. What can you do?" Child cries. Parent waits quietly or may say, "This upsets you," showing empathy without taking over. Child kicks ball and ball rolls out.

Had the mother thrust the breast into the child's mouth, had the father picked up the child regardless of the child's reaction, or had the parent given the doll or ball to the infant, these children would have been deprived of trying to handle the situation, learning by doing, and experiencing the joy of mastery. Trust your baby's competence: she wants to do things for herself, and she *can* do things for herself. You also know that your child needs help, but try to provide just that little amount of help that allows the child to take over again. Let him be the initiator and problem-solver. We can look at life as a continuation of conflicts or problems. The more often we have mastered a minute difficulty, the more capable we feel the next time.

Respect and autonomy in child care practices

Self-soothing

We know from literature as well as from observing infants, that they have a strong need for sucking from birth on. It is often referred to as the "sucking instinct" or "reflex." Sucking also stops crying. As a result, many crying children are given the breast or the bottle, not because they need food, but to end their crying. Thrusting the breast, the bottle, a pacifier or a teether into a crying infant's mouth is one of the most often used calming devices. It is fast, handy and it works. Sucking is an instinctual need and adults have an instinctual rather than objective reaction to it. When a mother says, "It makes me sick to see my five-year-old put his thumb in his mouth," or "How disgusting this two-year-old looks sucking on his blanket," it is obvious that deeper emotional layers in the parent are touched. Throughout history, thumb-sucking has aroused strong feelings. It was called a bad habit and was blamed for producing protruding teeth and a disobedient, withdrawn or insatiable child. Parents were advised to restrain the baby physically by tying its arms, pulling sleeves over its hands, using aluminum mittens or elbow splints, or putting something bitter-tasting on the thumbs. Gentler interferences have included pulling out the thumb, giving a substitute, and distracting, bribing, or showing dislike. Any of these reactions gives a child at a very early, impressionable age the message that something that feels so good, comforting, natural and easy is bad. It's like planting seeds of doubt and insecurity about one's own goodness or the goodness of the outside world. Some infants are born with their thumbs in their mouths or even have been known to suck in the womb. The thumb belongs to the infant. She has to discover it and learn how to use it as part of her own body. It is always available. It doesn't fall on the floor and get dirty or get lost when needed. The infant can put it in his mouth and pull it out according to his own needs and desires. In the process, he learns how to soothe himself and how to become self-reliant. When there is no misgiving about it, he will use it when and for as long as he really needs it. The development of the infant's independence is the very reason some parents frown on thumb-sucking.

I do not know when the pacifier was invented, but it is a very old device. It certainly made sense in times when infants were swaddled, rocked, and pacified. Common belief was that infants should be kept completely passive and helpless. They were prevented from having any activity and, indeed, became passive and quiet. In our days, pacifiers are given mainly for the following reasons: to stop crying, to meet the need for sucking, to put an infant to sleep, to soothe colic and to prevent thumb-sucking. The pacifier is a plug. It does stop a child from crying, but the question is, does an infant have a right to cry? Should an infant be allowed to express her feelings and communicate them? By plugging her mouth, the message given is, "Don't do what comes naturally. Do what pleases me, your parent. I am in control of how you should feel and how you should show your feelings." When anything is put into a young infant's mouth he starts sucking. However, is his real need for sucking met or is the pacifier given when parents' needs are interpreted as the infant's? When the pacifier is used to put an infant to sleep, it is often when the adult decides that the infant should sleep. In addition, there is no proof whatsoever that sucking the pacifier helps relieve colic better than sucking the thumb. Many parents prefer the pacifier to thumb-sucking. Why this fierce debate? What are the real or imagined dangers of thumb-sucking? Parents complain about being awakened many times in the night because the pacifier falls out of the baby's mouth. Yet they prefer this situation to one where the infant is in control. Some worry that the child will be sucking his or her thumb in kindergarten. Others claim they can always throw out the pacifier when the child becomes too old for it. Again, the parent is in control. The issue is not a simple preference of pacifier versus thumb. The real issue is who is in control?

Discipline

At RIE we certainly believe in the benefits of discipline, both for parents and infants. The word "discipline" has different meanings, both according to the dictionary and in people's minds. Parents often think of it as punishment, corporal or otherwise, or as a system of punishments and rewards. I see discipline as being a social contract, in which family (or community) members agree to accept and obey a particular set of rules. We need discipline just as we need traffic signs, and we have a mutual expectation that these red, yellow, and green lights will be observed in the same way by all members. Living within a system of generally accepted rules makes life easier for all of us. While rules vary among cultures and among families, I think most people would agree that a mutually acceptable system of rules is necessary for co-existence. This system can be determined within each family by clarifying the needs of its members, and then developing a set of rules or guidelines that accommodates those needs as much as possible. After deciding on the rules, a parent must then introduce them to the child and reinforce them. The question is, how? My guidelines for the "how" are as follows:

- Establish a few, simple, reasonable rules and make sure they are age-appropriate.

- Expect these rules to be obeyed.

- Be consistent but not rigid.

- Give the child choices within a secure framework.

- Remember that even children (especially children) need to be able to save face and avoid power struggles.

Let me talk about each one of these guidelines. First of all, remember that discipline is not a set of rigidly enforced mandates, but a process in which the child learns to become a social being. Social learning, like any other form of learning, is dependent upon the child's capacities. Don't expect things of a child that are against the very nature of their current develop-mental stage. To expect a newborn not to cry, a very young baby not to put things in her mouth, or a toddler not to say "no" is unreasonable. Also, timing is an important factor. One can't expect cooperation from a sleepy or hungry baby.

The second guideline also concerns expectations. In my practice I have seen that a child's response to parental demands depends very much upon the parents' own deep down expectations. The way a demand is expressed triggers the child to do something or not to do it. If the parent doesn't really believe in the validity of a particular rule, or is afraid that the child will not obey, the chances are that the child won't.

The third guideline calls for consistency. Predictability is habit-forming, and the forming of habits makes it much easier to live with rules. There are some things we don't need or want to re-examine every time we do them, such as brushing our teeth. It's much more convenient for us if actions like these become second nature. Because very young children do not understand the reasons behind the rules they are expected to follow, it is better if these rules become simply a matter of course. For example, it is much easier to get a baby to go to sleep when the same schedule and routine precedes each night's bedtime. This should continue until the child himself indicates the need for some sort of change. In addition, we all know how difficult it is to change habits once we have them. For this reason alone, we should try to establish good habits from the very beginning. This is why I tell parents to start establishing patterns and routines right from the child's birth. Through regular routines, babies eventually learn to anticipate what is expected of them. This is the beginning of discipline.

The fourth guideline refers to choice within boundaries. Boundaries that are predictably and consistently reinforced provide security. In order to really develop inner discipline, children must be given the freedom to make choices. Knowing when to give infants freedom and when to introduce limits is most important, and is the backbone of the RIE approach. We need to remember that limits function as traffic signals, keeping things flowing smoothly between family members. Within this framework are those things a child is expected to do (non-negotiable areas), what she is allowed to do (negotiable areas), what is tolerated ("I don't really like that, but I can understand why you need to do it"), and what is forbidden.

These are the parameters of discipline. Within these parameters are what I perceive as being inviolable areas of choice. Babies have an inborn capacity to make healthful choices about how they want to move and learn. They should be provided with safe, appropriately sized rooms in which they can move and explore freely. Their use of objects and play materials should not be restricted, governed, or overly interfered with. Babies must have freedom of choice in the area of gross motor development and manipulation. One can further enhance the child's sense of herself as a decision-maker by allowing enough time to elapse after requesting something, so that the child can decide on her own whether or not to cooperate.

This leads to the fifth guideline. If a child spends hours playing uninterruptedly, he will be much more willing to cooperate with the demands of his parent. If he doesn't have to fight for autonomy, he can comfortably relinquish it once in a while. And we must understand that children need to be able to save face when they have not obeyed a rule. Children fight an inner struggle. One part of them wants to please, yet they also have to resist in order to test the limits of their power. In a way, each one of us carries around that eternal two-year-old, who shouts "no" as he is offered an ice-cream cone, even while reaching for it. None of us really likes to be told what to do, even when it is good for us.

In our parent–infant guidance classes, we like to model how we teach and reinforce rules. We have a snack for the older babies at a special table, around which the demonstrator and the babies sit. Children may choose between items to eat and drink, and may choose not to have a snack, but they may not take food, juice, or bottles away from the table. It is an incredible learning experience for all of us to see how even the youngest infants learn the rule and decide whether or not to obey it. After many repetitions of the rule, they get the message and then have to test it over and over again. We've often seen a baby or toddler steal away from the table and then turn back to make sure that the demonstrator sees her, as though she were checking to see whether the rule would be enforced. This shows that the child understands that a rule exists. It is natural for children to carry food away from the table. They can see no real reason not to. When a child ignores the rule, the demonstrator tries to show that she fully understands the child's desire to do what he wants, and that he is not naughty or bad for having that desire. Therefore, she does not get angry with the child, but calmly and unemotionally repeats the rule. Of course, we understand parents who get irritated when their toddlers play with the television set after being told "no" several times. But it becomes easier to handle once one realizes that the child's behavior stems from a natural inclination and not from a desire to drive the parent crazy.

The RIE approach to discipline is not permissive, but understanding. Children, like adults, need rules and guidelines. I conceptualize discipline as being a system based on and facilitating mutual respect among family members. We could easily exchange the word "discipline" for the word "educaring" – they are both a combination of learning and nurturing. The goal is inner or self-discipline, self-confidence, and joy in the act of cooperation.

RIE practices

Parent–infant guidance classes

When parents come for the first time to RIE parent–infant guidance classes, they generally bring with them certain needs and expectations. First of all, parents come to the classes with a very understandable need to commiserate with each other on the joys, trials, and tribulations of parenthood and infancy. It would come naturally to parents to want to casually sit down with babes-in-arms and begin to discuss the best diapering service, places to buy baby paraphernalia, and how to get their babies to *go to sleep*.

Of course, parents should be given or make for themselves plenty of opportunity to get together and share resources, ideas, information, feelings, and support. We at RIE would like to see parent support happen as a by-product of our classes, but it is not our main purpose. Our classes are designed to be infant as well as adult-oriented, in that we focus on the infant's initiations, needs and cues, demonstrating sensitive and appropriate ways of responding to them. We try to model ways in which the needs of infants and parents can be synchronized. We believe this will help parents more in the long run than if we were to emphasize solely parent-support activities. Many parents also bring with them the expectation that they will receive quick and ready explanations and solutions about parenting and infancy. In our hectic world the standard way to learn about anything is to pick up a "how-to" book on a given subject and start reading, or to go to a class and have the instructor tell us what to do. In my opinion, this is short-term learning, and it usually doesn't work.

RIE parent–infant classes, by their very nature, rely on and encourage long-term learning. Our classes are eight weeks long. Effective parenting cannot be learned or "taught" in eight weeks. The goal in our classes is for parents to observe and really see their infants. The classes are divided into two sections. In the first, parents ease their infants into a prepared environment, then move back to a spot where they can sit quietly and watch as the RIE demonstrator interacts with the infants. We ask parents to try to remain in the same place throughout the observation period, so that their babies will always be able to find them. This gives the babies the requisite security they need in order to move away from their parents, accept the attention of the demonstrator, and get involved in exploring the environment and the other infants. The fact that the parent is there allows the baby to let go of the parent. The RIE demonstrator will meanwhile pay full attention to the babies, responding to their cues, and helping them either directly or by not helping them. With her soft voice and slow movements she will try to create an atmosphere of peace and quiet. After observation of about one hour, the RIE instructor will lead a parent discussion to talk over issues that have arisen during the class as well as at home.

It is difficult to relinquish the primary caregiving role, even for an hour. It is difficult to operate without a curriculum or constant instruction. It is difficult to believe that one can be a good parent simply by sitting and watching. In asking parents to accept this different mode of parenting, we are asking a lot. The first few classes of each session reflect these difficulties. Parents are tense, somewhat confused, not quite knowing how to behave or what to think. But even in the very short span of eight weeks, a noticeable change occurs. The parents and babies become more comfortable and acclimated – more relaxed. At this point, as if by osmosis, long-term learning – deeper and subtler than any quick retention of facts – begins to take place.

I also know how pressured parents are, by all the magazines, the media and other parents, to do something to stimulate learning in their infants. On one occasion, Dr. Pikler and I visited one of those "baby swim" classes. There were about 15 mothers and a few fathers there with babies from four to eight months old. Although the instructor explained that the purpose of the class was not to teach the infants how to swim, but simply to help them learn to enjoy the water, and reminded the parents not to force their babies, he proceeded to instruct: "Now jump up. Take them under the water. Make the baby kick." The speed, the excitement, the up and down, didn't take into account the babies' or parents' timing. To me it felt like an army drill. It made me increasingly uncomfortable to see the delighted smiles of the parents. For them, the excitement and fun seemed contagious. The babies, however, looked scared and surprised. Some were bewildered. At times a few cried. Yet the parents kept saying, "Isn't it fun?" Only one mother, of an apparently exhausted baby, said, "I think that is enough for you," and picked the baby up and rested her on the side of the pool.

All these parents were loving, caring people. Yet they listened to the instructor and reinforced each other with, "Aren't the babies having fun?" They neither looked at the babies' faces nor seemed to see or read their children's feelings. What did these babies really learn or experience? The parents enjoyed being together and needed to reinforce each other in their belief that they were doing the right thing for their infants. They wanted to believe that their babies were learning. They needed to feel confident. My advice is: to gain confidence, look at your baby. Respond to your baby. Enjoy what your baby is doing right now. If you want to give your infant a positive experience, take clues from your own observations. While these classes offer support and companionship to parents, the babies (in order to attend these classes) must be interrupted during their natural rhythms of sleep and play, then restricted in infant seats while in the car. They are exposed to a barrage of people and activities and expected to conform to an externally imposed curriculum. I recommend that parents form small groups in which their babies are the "actors" and "scriptwriters." The parents can then watch, learn, and enjoy.

During the RIE parent–infant classes we are trying to impart a quality of experience – a way of relating that can be used at all levels of growth. In the long run, our goal is to help parents learn to live and let live with their infants and later their older children. Such insight cannot be measured by the hours spent in class or the number of pages read. Long-term learning is a slow process: a timed-release awareness that takes more than eight weeks to gestate. It must happen organically – allowing for time in which the seeds of understanding may sprout, grow, bloom, and bear fruit.

Group care for infants and toddlers

As an infant advocate over several decades, I have witnessed many changes in attitudes towards infant care in general and towards group care in particular. Until recently, the care of infants in the US has largely been the concern of the family and the family physician. Since the 1950s, the need for providing alternative care has become increasingly apparent. In the 1950s, group care of infants was non-existent and looked upon as potentially harmful. In the 1960s, the pros and cons of group care were debated in an emotionally loaded atmosphere. In the 1970s an increasing number of infants spent six, eight, or more hours each weekday in group care. State and federal regulations, even when met, do not insure that the infants' needs are met too.

In my work of consulting with a great variety of centers, I have found that, while the people in charge of infant centers are usually well-meaning, child-loving people who want to do a decent job, this is rarely possible because of the low pay and status of the infant caregiver, poor (if any) pre- and in-service training, very few model centers, inadequate facilities, constant changes in personnel, and so forth. Can any center meet the needs of infants under such difficult conditions? What are the infants' needs, beyond those for food, rest, warmth and hygiene? Most people would respond with the following: love, as demonstrated by rocking, fondling and body contact, and cognitive stimulation, as demonstrated by an abundance of objects, teaching materials and lesson plans. These needs have become largely accepted and most centers try to meet them in different ways.

We who follow the RIE philosophy have our own ways of meeting infants' needs. We focus on two areas of the infant's life: the time spent with the adult who cares for the infant and the time the infant spends alone, freely exploring his environment. Only a child who receives undivided attention from his educarer during all routine caregiving activities will be free and interested to explore his environment without needing too much intervention from the educarer. If the educarer understands that the infant needs both concentrated attention while being cared for, and time to explore alone, she or he also gains time for herself or himself.

In order to highlight the differences between the attitude of a good average caregiver and a trained educarer, I will compare and contrast the two.

Whereas a caregiver may rush through routine caring activities in order to get ready for the more valued time of following a curriculum, lesson plan, or providing some structured stimulation, the educarer uses the time that must be spent with the child anyway as a potential source of valued learning experience.

Whereas many caregivers rely on infant curricula, books and packaged programs as a prescription to teach, drill and speed up new skills in the areas of gross motor, fine motor, social/emotional or language development, the educarer trusts the infants' abilities to initiate their own activities, choose from available objects, and work on their own projects without interruption.

Whereas the caregiver teaches and encourages postures and means of locomotion that the infants are not yet able to do on their own (thus hampering free movement and exploration and sometimes even creating bodily discomfort), the educarer provides appropriate space for the infant to freely initiate his own movements without interference, thus helping the infant feel comfortable, competent and self-reliant.

Whereas the caregiver's attention is focused on the elicited response to her or his stimulation, the educarer focuses upon observing the whole child, his reaction to the caregiving person, to the environment, and to his peers, thus learning about the child's personality and needs.

Whereas the caregiver selects and puts objects/toys in the infants' hands, the educarer places the objects/toys so the infant must make an effort to reach and grasp. The child works towards what she or he wants.

Whereas the caregiver encourages dependency by assuming an active role, such as rescuing a child in distress or helping her to solve her problems, the educarer waits to see if the child is capable of consoling himself and solving his own problems, thus encouraging autonomy.

Whereas the caregiver may often use bottles and/or pacifiers to soothe a crying child, creating a false oral need for food and sucking, the educarer accepts the child's right to show both positive and negative feelings. The educarer does not want to stop the crying, but rather she or he tries to understand and attend to the child's real needs, such as sleeplessness, hunger or cold. If the infant soothes himself by sucking his thumb, the educarer accepts this as a positive, self-comforting activity.

Whereas the caregiver often restricts infant–infant interaction, such as infants touching each other, for fear of them hurting each other, the educarer facilitates interactions by closely observing, in order to know when to intervene and when not to.

Whereas, in a situation of conflict between infants, the caregiver resolves the problem by separating, distracting, or deciding who should have the toy or object in question, the educarer would comment, "Both you,

John, and you, Anne, want that toy." Often, after such impartial comments, minor conflicts resolve themselves.

Whereas the caregiver may become aggressive in controlling an "aggressor," thereby reinforcing the aggressive behavior, the educarer models appropriate behavior by touching the aggressive child and quietly saying something like, "Easy, gentle...nice."

Whereas the caregiver may rush to pick up, to rescue and to console the "victim" of the "aggressor", the educarer squats down, touches and strokes the "victim" saying, "Gently now, nice." By concurrently stroking and talking to both the "victim" and the "aggressor," the educarer is modeling and consoling both children without reinforcing a pattern of becoming a "victim."

Whereas the caregiver likes to have more people or helpers in the room, the educarer wants to become the steady person to his or her own small group of about four infants.

Whereas the caregiver gets exhausted from picking up one crying child and putting down another, as if extinguishing one fire after another, the educarer calmly observes and can often prevent the "fire."

Whereas the caregiver may scoop up an infant unexpectedly from behind, thereby startling, interrupting and creating resistance in the infant, the educarer always tells the infant before she or he does anything with him or her, and thus gets cooperation.

All of these examples illustrate that while both the caregiver and the educarer love the infant, the educarer demonstrates love by showing and teaching respect.

Chapter 3

The RIE Early Years "Curriculum"

Ruth Money

Our role is to create an environment in which the child can do all the things the child would do naturally. The misleading thing about this is that it sounds so easy.

Magda Gerber

Introduction

The goal of RIE is to improve the quality of infant care in any setting: home, day care, hospital and parent–infant groups. My experience comes from being the founder and director of the first RIE Demonstration Infant Center, the South Bay Infants Center (SBIC), in Redondo Beach, California. This was founded in 1988, and was in operation for ten years. My goal was to establish a working model to demonstrate it was possible to give high quality, individual care to each infant in a day care center adhering to the principles of the Pikler/RIE philosophy. In fact, we showed that it is not only possible but also easier than offering a poor service (Money 1992).

Infants attending the SBIC came from families where both parents worked. Since we were committed to providing continuity of care for the infants for two years, the center appealed to parents and staff members who wanted that kind of stability. The children entered aged about three months and left aged about 27 months. Most were full term and healthy. We also acted as a mainstream setting for some disabled infants, although no more than one child in a group of four. We developed methods for infant day care based on the philosophy and experiences of Emmi Pikler and Magda

Gerber and demonstrated how these could be translated into a program forming the basis of an early years "curriculum."

However, an "RIE curriculum" within an infant center is not merely a list of activities aimed at teaching things to the babies. The "curriculum" is rather the style of care offered during the course of the infants' everyday life at the center. The method is called "educaring," a term coined by Magda Gerber (Gerber 1998, p.1), that means educating infants while caring for them, by seeing and responding to each infant as a person with unique needs. It emphasizes the interdependent relationship between educating and caring for babies. The RIE approach was based on observations by Magda Gerber of infants in all sorts of contexts, including programs at the Dubnoff School (1968–71) (Gerber 1971) and the Demonstration Infant Program (DIP)(1972–1976) (Gerber 2000, p.69). In both, enrolment was open to children without additional needs, as well as high-risk and distressed infants from birth to 18 months (Gerber 2000, pp.81–2). The philosophy Magda Gerber brought to the US was not just the principle of respect for infants, an idea with which hardly anyone would disagree, but experience in the practice of how to implement, demonstrate and explain respect for infants. Gerber focused her attention on young, pre-verbal children and helped parents observe and see the competencies and needs of the young infant. Infant competency was largely unnoticed by parents and professionals alike in the US culture of the 1950s.

The social context began to change from the 1960s onwards, when a growing wave of mothers of young children began to join the workforce, and out of home care grew rapidly in the US. Free public kindergartens for all five-year-olds were becoming common, and private nursery schools were also becoming popular, on a part-time basis, for a growing number of middle class pre-school children from three to five. In the 1970s, Head Start was founded as a summer program to help five-year-olds from socio-economically disadvantaged families and it grew to be a huge year-round free program serving four-year-olds (Hymes 1991, pp.1–2). By this time, different philosophies and methods of educating and communicating with nursery school children over three years old were competing with one another in the US. Nursery schools were open to children who were verbal and toilet trained and settings generally considered to be of high quality were based on child-centered goals for social and emotional development and reading readiness. Yet there were others that advocated highly structured, teacher-directed, skills-acquisition curricula (Hymes 1991, p.357). In contrast, infant care out of the home was almost non-existent and the idea of reciprocal communication with infants was also practically unheard of. In fact the Latin word "infans" means "unable to speak" (*New Shorter Oxford*

English Dictionary 1993). However, as mothers of younger and younger children went into the workforce, infant care in out of home settings grew.

Gerber's focus of interest was communication with small children by observing and responding to the cues of infants up to the age of two years. This included toddlers who could walk but were not yet able to communicate effectively by speech. Up to two years of age is also the legal definition used by the state of California in its licensing regulations for infants, a term which includes babies and young toddlers. As detailed elsewhere (see Chapter 1), Dr. Tom Forrest invited Gerber to come to the Children's Health Council in Palo Alto, California to co-direct the Demonstration Infant Program (DIP) in 1972. As part of this work they also began to make presentations at conferences sponsored by the state and the National Association for the Education of Young Children. This was a timely development, as early childhood educators were becoming more interested in caring for infants in groups, in order to meet the demand for day care created as more mothers of young children entered the workforce. Gerber stressed the importance of observing each infant, responding to her/him with respect, developing an "authentic" relationship (see Glossary) with a very young child, and using caregiving as an important part of the curriculum. Her approach was a striking alternative to the more common response to infant day care: to water down the pre-school curriculum. Gerber based her methods on the care she had observed at the Loczy Institute in Budapest, where the children had been cared for in a manner that had also been considered unusual in Europe at that time (Falk 1986).

The following chapter will outline the nature of the RIE early years "curriculum," which is based on the philosophy of respect for infants and the development of infant care using reciprocal relationships guided by observing and responding to the baby's cues. Finally, an analysis of RIE principles and practices will show how the RIE philosophy of respect, developed by Magda Gerber and based on the work of Emmi Pikler, can be adopted within different infant care settings.

The RIE "curriculum"

The RIE "curriculum" is derived from the model that Emmi Pikler developed at the Loczy residential program for infants. Her work continued and developed under the subsequent directorship of Judit Falk (Falk 1986) and currently continues under directorship of Pikler's daughter, Anna Tardos. The SBIC adapted this model to day care, and also incorporated an additional dimension of developing respectful parent relationships, education and support derived from Magda Gerber's work. We found that this added dimension needs to be an integral part of infant care. Indeed, it is critical where care of the infant is shared by parents and caregivers. In summary the four principles of Loczy (see Chapter 1), applied by Gerber to appropriate curriculum (Gerber 1979) plus an additional fifth principle needed in the day care context are as follows:

- The value of self-initiated activity of children from their earliest age.

- The value of building a trusting relationship with a consistent, professional caregiver whose attitudes are directed by respect for the child's personality and understanding of his needs.

- The value of sustaining each child in building self-awareness. This is done through encouraging active participation in whatever is going on – alone or in interaction – rather than simply perceiving the child as an object to be cleaned and fed.

- The value of fostering optimal health in the children, reciprocally influenced by the first three points.

- The value of respectful connection and communication between professional caregiver and parents as crucial to the current and continuing life of the child.

Pikler and Gerber also introduced the concept of providing a stable routine that was predictable by the infant, and this was also an important element in the SBIC program. In putting these principles into practice at the SBIC, we kept in mind Gerber's advice: "Appropriate curriculum for infants should not be a special teaching plan added to their daily activities, but rather it should be incorporated in the infants' every experience" (Gerber 1979b, p.84). At the SBIC we found that treating an infant in this way in everyday life completely changes the nature of the relationship between adults and children, and adults did indeed come to see infants through new eyes. An infant center can provide an appropriate learning environment for children through fostering the development of a respectful relationship between the primary caregiver and each infant or toddler. However, this must be in the context of respectful relationships between adults, as well as between an adult carer and an infant.

Parents continue to be the most important ongoing influence in an infant's life as he grows up. The center works to establish and maintain respectful relationships both with parents and among members of the staff in order to foster the infants' attachment to both. The center can also provide a safe space where infants can learn to move as freely and as naturally as animals do. RIE offers clear insights into how to respond individually to the increasing abilities of each infant in small groups throughout their developmental stages of infancy and toddlerhood. All of the above elements of a RIE-based early years "curriculum" will be discussed below in greater detail.

Building a respectful relationship

RIE builds on the foundation of establishing a respectful relationship between the infant and a primary carer, and also with a few other significant adults who form a stable part of the baby's life. Within the relationship, RIE encourages the adult to become acquainted with the non-verbal infant through sensitive observation of the child's cues, and to offer both security and freedom to the infant within the relationship.

In order to achieve RIE's basic goal of improving the quality of infant care in any setting, the first step is to establish a chain of respectful relationships. In the home, the key link is between baby and parents. In an early years setting, the key link is between the infant and a primary caregiver but the chain extends to other staff, to the parents (who are the child's most important and ongoing support throughout life) and to other significant adults who form a stable part of the infant's life. Whether in a natural family or a day care center, RIE's practice aims to create an environment where each individual is respected (see Figure 3.1). The additional insights that RIE practitioners have brought to the Loczy method include this way of relating the approach to day care settings, where the babies may spend a large part of their day, but where their natural parents are still the primary caregivers. The

Figure 3.1 An environment in which each individual is respected

central relationship model is characterized by the more powerful and capable adult treating the baby with careful regard for his uniqueness, seeds of autonomy, and competence. The method demands "authenticity," with the more mature adult accepting the emotions of the child, and being honest with the child. The respectful adult has an appreciation for what the baby can already do in the strange new world into which he has been born: to breathe air, take in food, eliminate, cry, recognize his mother's voice, and respond to the environment. RIE points out that the competency of pre-verbal infants is often unnoticed, maybe because in many respects the infant's very survival is dependent upon the care of adults. Essential to best practice is comprehensive knowledge of the little recognized stages of natural motor development in infants.

Gerber's principles were geared to providing infants with what they needed, and she gave very practical demonstrations of these through down-to-earth teaching of specific situations and responses between infants and adults, and infants and infants. For example, in relation to motor development, she would demonstrate by having adults either watch a videotape or observe a baby in her parent–infant classes. She would point out, or have a parent note, the strain and lack of grace in a baby who was put into a position she could not achieve by herself or, more often, to admire the agility, grace and efficiency of movement that an infant initiated in order to reach a position or a toy that she wanted. She helped people see the good judgment that self-motivated infants used to keep themselves safe. The approach is rooted in the unique insights that Pikler had pioneered on the advantages of allowing natural gross motor development, an approach that differed markedly from that of mainstream American researchers in infant development who used, and still often use today, diagnostic milestones for pediatric medical examination as a model for raising babies. For example, medical developmental charts show that at the median age of 7.3 months, an infant who is pulled up to a sitting position by the examining physician can maintain this position (*Manual for the Bayley Scales of Infant Development*; Psychological Corporation, 1969). Experts accepted, and parents believed, that they should exercise their baby by pulling her into a sitting position. Gerber supported optimal gross motor development by allowing and encouraging the intrinsically motivated natural movement that Pikler had documented and demonstrated over the years at Loczy (Pikler 1971, pp. 54–89). An accurate reference for use in setting expectations for normal, healthy, physical development is offered by the charming drawings by Klara Pap in Pikler's charts of natural gross motor development (Pikler 1971, pp. 70–71). There are no milestones to accomplish by a certain time in these charts, taken from life drawings. The quality of the movement is valued rather than the age at which it is accomplished.

While Gerber was explicit in explaining natural infant development and children's needs, she also gave the adults, students, practitioners and parents, the time and support they needed. This was modeled through the relationships that developed naturally around the care of the baby, rather than through formal teaching or lecturing. Magda Gerber believed strongly that effective teaching comes through demonstration and internalization of ways of working (see Chapter 7).

Because the inborn competence of infants to learn to move without propping or assistance has been so little noted in other approaches to infant care and development, these natural developmental stages will be described in detail later in this chapter.

Independence and interdependence

RIE fosters caregiving that supports safety and exploration in *both* physical and psychological domains, since the infant needs to develop both *interdependence* and *independence*. Human beings have to grow in competence as they mature, but if babies are only seen as totally dependent, their innate competence is not appreciated and then adult caring will be *for* not *with* the baby. There will be no expectation that the baby can help in the caring activity and the adult may well find it easier and quicker to do things herself. However, such a mindset may not serve the infant well in the long run and the RIE approach suggests it is crucial to slow down and to observe at any particular moment what a baby is doing. At that moment of focused attention it can be seen what a baby can do for herself. As RIE's purpose is to foster the development of healthy, competent, cooperative, creative children, taking an infant's need for both *interdependence* and *independence* into consideration, a model of a *cooperative* relationship must be adopted from the beginning of the infant/adult relationship. Perhaps, initially, the more powerful adult needs to furnish 99 per cent of the cooperation and the baby only 1 per cent. However, observing the baby's growing competence in social interactions will enable a little more cooperative engagement. A good example of this principle in practice is the diapering, described by Gerber in *The RIE Manual for Parents and Professionals* (Gerber 2000, p.39).

In this way, the RIE model for interdependence can grow as the baby matures and can do more and more, and the adult can grow to become more sensitive and aware of each baby and her individual cues. Signs of the infant's growing competence may not only be unnoticed and unappreciated by the adult, but even thwarted if the old model of "baby as dependent" remains. And if the infant does not see recognition of her competence reflected in the adult's eyes, then it could go unnoticed and unappreciated by the infant herself. Opportunities for the adult to grow in understanding and responsive behavior may pass by as well, and activities can become routine rather than enjoyable and will certainly become more difficult than if the baby is a willing participant.

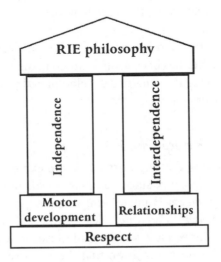

Figure 3.2 The two pillars of RIE Copyright © Patty Ryan 2001

Building independence

As discussed earlier, gross motor behavior is one of the first areas in which a young baby naturally gains competence. Pikler's research demonstrated that infants are endowed by nature with the ability to learn to move, to sit, to stand and to walk, without being taught (Pikler 1971, pp. 54–89). In fact, interfering with a baby's natural pace of development is detrimental to the optimal acquisition of her motor skills (Pikler 1994, pp. 5–6). Interference has a negative effect on the qualities of grace, surety, and the child's sensory awareness of her own movements. In addition, development of initiative, judgment, coping skills and satisfaction in controlling one's own efforts are rooted in early, natural, unassisted motor development supported by a safe environment and a secure relationship (Pikler 1994, pp. 5–6).

The usual stages of gross motor development attained by babies, starting from a supine position on their backs (a position recommended by RIE), begins with head turning, then moving the arms and hands, kicking the legs and then rolling a little to the side. After a baby becomes more and more secure in a side-lying position, the next stage will be rolling right over onto the belly. From there the infant will return from the belly to the back again, although often her first attempts are unsuccessful, sometimes because one hand has become stuck under her body. If the infant is becoming fussy or tired, the educarer will talk to her, and then gently roll her back to her original position on her back so she can try again. The infant spends the next few months lying on the belly stretching and rolling, eventually coming to crawl on the belly and then later creeping on all fours, and at this point an infant will usually attempt to stand. Different infants do this in different ways. Some will come to a half-sitting position and then will sit, some initially on their knees, and then, using the sole of one foot for support, will stand up. "However, every movement in this process demands weeks or months of practice, like all the other sequences" (Pikler 1994, p.9). Infants will attain sitting positions by their own efforts and will learn to balance, to sit comfortably and with good posture. They will pull themselves up to stand and will cruise around upright holding onto something. Infants have to be able to balance in order to stand without support and, once this has been accomplished, will soon be able to walk alone. These stages of gross motor development proceed naturally as the infant's muscles and nerves mature in a head to toe direction, and from the spine outward. The infant's internal cues are based on feedback from sensory nerves within the muscles of the body as well as the five senses. For infants to move with grace, efficacy and sensory awareness, they must be permitted their own timetable. In general, it is favorable for infants such as those born prematurely or who are delayed for various reasons, to experience success in what they can do at their own speed rather than to be put in uncomfortable postures more advanced than their developmental level (Pikler 1971, p.79). Gerber did not focus on finding a problem and fixing it, but rather on discovering and pointing out areas of competency and then fostering successes upon which the infant could build more competence.

Basing practice on Pikler's analysis of the process of intrinsic self-motivated motor development (Pikler 1994, pp.5–13), RIE allows infants' physical development to proceed naturally from the earliest times by holding them or placing them in the position of greatest stability and greatest mobility, that is, on their backs. Their heavy head and weak neck, as well as their trunk, are supported. They can breathe freely, move their arms and legs and turn their heads in comfort. To foster natural development, the adult provides a completely safe environment, the characteristics of which will be discussed later in the chapter, which is available if needed by the infant. The adult observes subtleties of movement and response in order to understand the infant's competencies and needs. The early tonic neck reflex (see Glossary) is involuntary in a young infant placed on his back, when he turns his head to look at his fist in a horizontal fencing position. He shifts his body and his gaze from one side to another. These reflexive movements will reduce in time, but the exercise forms the basis for his later eye–hand co-ordination that will be under his voluntary control. Safe, appropriate equipment, described below, is provided so they will not be hindered as inner processes drive them to turn over, roll, crawl, creep, sit, stand and walk on their own schedule. The infants find the success of their effort self-rewarding. The quality of the movement is considered more important than the date at which a milestone is attained. The infant's independent, self-initiated motor activity also develops eye–hand co-ordination, eye–foot co-ordination, dexterity, bodily awareness, good posture, and judgment of how to move safely. Allowing such freedom within the secure relationship importantly allows the child to develop favorable emotional and intellectual abilities, and coping skills that influence personality development.

Infants also need freedom in their play. In a RIE setting they are furnished with simple, open-ended "toys" (see Chapter 5) and are respected while they are engaged in their play. Adults try not to interrupt and, if interruption is necessary, do it in a courteous and considerate manner. More dexterous and complex play results when infants solve these spatial, non-verbal problems for themselves. They learn not only how to move, but also how to navigate across the room to reach a favorite object, and how to use an object in a variety of ways. These early coping skills correlate with an optimistic, self-confident attitude toward solving problems. RIE values freedom of emotion as well as of motion, accepting the full range of a child's feelings with equanimity. In time, the child can come to recognize them, and be able to deal with them in a constructive way. As Jackins has argued, crying is not the hurt, it is the release or healing of the hurt (Jackins 1965, pp.76–81). Clearly, in "authentic" relationships it is important to acknowledge infants when they are sad or angry, as well as when they are happy and cheerful. But, although emotions are accepted, limits are placed on behavior. A toddler might be very upset if her ball goes into the street. It is possible to acknowledge her feelings, "I can see you really want the ball and don't like that it went outside the fence," but still say, "I will not let you go in the street to get it, that is not safe." The adult should not distract her from processing feelings, but stay available until she finishes crying. In a day care situation, parents are encouraged to have unhurried time with their child before they leave but then, rather than sneak away, say goodbye. If the child cries, they are not hushed up, rather the primary caregiver acknowledges the tears but reassures the child that the parents will return. The educarer looks for cues and responds with the degree of comfort that matches the level of comfort needed by the child, perhaps staying close by or giving a touch or a hug.

Most often, the infant who has been emotionally "refueled" (see Glossary) by a time with the parent in the center before she leaves will turn contentedly to the playroom.

Infants also need freedom to try to do their own problem-solving in infant–infant interactions, as long as they are not hurting one another. Their sense of fairness is not that of an adult, yet they often work out situations satisfactorily to suit themselves. Piaget (1975) theorizes that the organizing principles of the moral development of a child are different from those of the adult world. The organization and reorganization of the cognitive structures of morality in the first years have underlying biological bases. It is not efficient or realistic to try to get infants to share, for example, before they have developed the cognitive and emotional structure to do so. If an educarer senses that the situation might escalate, she intervenes in the smallest way possible. Initially, this may be to move closer in a gentle, peaceful way, then to "sports-cast" (describe aloud what each child is doing), and to stroke them gently, while telling them that she would like them to be gentle with one another. The educarer does not try to find out who had an object first, or to dictate the result, but will keep the maturing baby safe through the many stages of moral development in infancy. Infants progress through stages: recognizing the difference between self and others and gaining control of their own body, before becoming more interested in outside objects. Before the infant is interested in the ownership of an object, pleasure may be shown when another infant takes the object away. Desiring ownership of an object usually comes next. Later, the infant may progress from wanting something to be "mine," to an empathic state where sharing with other toddlers is desired. Infants also need freedom of speech – even to say "no." Because it is valuable for young children to be able to say "no," it is also important to avoid addressing them in a manner that might bring a negative response in a situation in which they really have no choice. For example, if their nappy needs to be changed, they can be offered the choice of walking to the changing table or being carried. This manner of treating the "terrible twos" (the period often associated with temper tantrums and negative responses) with respect can help avoid the tantrum behavior of a child who feels unheard. The developmental task of the very young child is to learn what he wants and needs. Later, maturity along with guidance and modeling will help in the acquisition of consideration for others' needs as well as of appropriate social skills. It is through such interactions that an infant hears and learns language, builds trust or mistrust, learns social skills and learns how to recognize and channel emotions.

Building interdependence

Responding to the infant's need for affiliation builds interdependence. The paradox of the complexity of human behavior is that even the freedom of motion and emotion offered to an infant is rooted in the relationship with an adult. It is the "authentic" relationship that gives the infant the security to be independent. It is the adult who makes the environment safe so that the infant can move in tune with his own body rhythms. It is the adult who makes the baby's life stable and predictable. It is the adult who appreciates that the infant is moving in keeping with his own inner spontaneous motivation, and reflects that appreciation back to the infant. It is the adult who incorporates and models authenticity, and fosters it in the child. So a respectful relationship accommodates the infant's need to be free, as well as the need for security and affiliation.

For example, the infant's self-initiation is incorporated in the caregiving interaction of feeding. The caregiver is in control of offering healthy food. She offers the bottle when the infant shows signs of hunger, and stops when he signals that he has had enough. In an older infant, she sits with him and offers a plate of very tiny servings. She feeds him and also allows him to feed himself simultaneously. She talks to him about what he is eating, asks if he wants more when a food is gone from his plate, and serves him a small amount more only as he asks for it. In this way, he is helped to learn to self-regulate his eating. This is also the procedure when a group of four young toddlers start having meals together at the same table.

RIE practice: the Seven Principles of Respect

(Gerber and Johnson 1998, pp.4–5)

Pikler's study of infants' capabilities and needs enabled her to develop and test practices that promote optimal development in infants and very young children. The knowledge of the infant gained through observation helps the adult to promote the child's independence and interdependence. The following seven practices are recommended as ways to promote quality care in any setting.

1. Basic trust in the child to be an initiator, an explorer, and a self-learner

The infant is capable of many self-initiated, self-motivated behaviors. If the adult does not realize this, how can she trust in the infant to behave in these ways? RIE teaches students to observe by providing a peaceful environment so that the infants themselves can demonstrate what they can do on their own. For an infant, the capacity for self-initiation, exploration and self-learning is especially evident in the area of gross motor development. Gross motor development is also the easiest thing to observe. When the progress over time in motor capabilities of an infant is pointed out to the observers, they can themselves become researchers. Educarers need to become aware of subtle stages of motor development early on, and to recognize and appreciate the mini-milestones between the predominant ones of sitting, standing and walking. As the observer continues to observe and to learn, based on personal experience, she builds basic trust in the infant's ability to initiate, explore, and learn from doing. As infants get older, it is possible to see judgment about safety grow with the developing motor skills. Observation of older babies reveals language development and social development, and research has shown that infants have a built-in capacity to acquire language naturally, as self-learners in an environment where language is spoken (Eliot 1999, pp.351–2; Pinker 1994; Ward 2000). In interactions with a non-verbal infant or a toddler just learning to speak, it is more respectful to have a conversation by talking to them about their concerns, rather than trying to teach them about things that are not a part of their life. And it is more courteous for the adult to offer words in a conversational tone, for instance, to talk about the pink rose you are viewing together, rather than quiz the child on "What color is that?" Questions to a child are best confined to situations where information is truly needed.

2. An environment for the child that is physically safe, cognitively challenging, and emotionally nurturing

By physically safe, Gerber meant providing an environment that was so safe that even if the infant or infants were by some catastrophe left unattended for a day, they would be unhurt, even if hungry or dirty or miserable. This applied to the physical environment, by providing safe toys and equipment geared to the size and ability of the child as well as having gated areas, covered electrical outlets, and so on. For an infant who is just learning to crawl, a climbing structure should only be two inches high, so that if the baby falls off, there will be no serious harm, but the event will be a learning experience. During these stages of rapid motor development in infants, we gradually make available equipment that is more challenging while still being safe: steps, climbing structures, slides, etc. and also larger spaces in which to move.

To be physically safe in a day care center, RIE advocates having only a few infants of the same developmental level in a stable group together. Toddlers who have not yet developed good judgment, for example, may be curious to investigate a younger baby's eyes. Infants in a familiar environment with their developmental peers, who have been free to move their bodies in keeping with their natural motor development, learn to maneuver peacefully around one another, even if their chronological age is different. For example at the RIE center, a tiny one-year-old girl with dismorphia (a medical condition in which a person has one or more unusual physical features) who could not yet roll over by herself was put in a group with three other infants who were three months old. She started to move and became more mobile than the infants in the group. By the time she was three years old, she was walking, talking and playing with the gentlest children in her age group (Pinto 2001, pp.1,5 and 6).

For cognitive challenge, RIE provides passive toys for active children, toys that need to be acted upon for a reaction to happen, not vice versa. Simple, open-ended toys are also less expensive than complicated, busy boxes and electronic gadgets. Busy toys provide infants with very few choices: push this button and a clown pops up, pull this lever and a song plays. Infants cannot stop a pre-programed toy, even if the noise or action is over-stimulating or bothersome. We offer simple objects such as a sturdy cotton scarf that an infant can maneuver even with a palmar grasp (see Glossary), empty plastic bottles or lightweight colanders that an infant can lift and look through. For mobile infants, we provide buckets, purses and objects to dump, put back in and carry around. As the children mature, we bring out stacking toys and nesting cups, blocks, more dolls and stuffed animals, manipulative objects to use in any way they choose. Such objects have unlimited possibilities for use by the developing child, and even in our teddy bears there are no hidden noisemakers that may confuse an infant.

By "emotionally nurturing," RIE is referring to responsive care within a respectful relationship that includes cooperative, responsive, dependable caregiving from a few familiar persons who permit the child to explore, beginning with the earliest sensory-motor development. The familiar, ongoing people in an infant's world can include parents and primary care-givers who offer continuity of care during the first years of life. It is impor-tant that the adult is available and accepting of a child's feelings in angry and sad times as well as happy ones. Elizabeth Memel expresses it in her phrase of "time in" with a misbehaving child rather than "time out" (Memel 1996, pp. 1 and 6–7). A child needs to feel that help and comfort is available not only in distress, but that they are also secure and loved when they are active and occupied, creative and problem-solving.

3. Time for uninterrupted play

The educarer does not interrupt when the baby is actively occupied in play. The same respect should be practiced when approaching a baby as when approaching an adult who is engrossed in reading a newspaper. If it is not an emergency, the educarer can sit down close by and observe. If the infant looks up, she sees the adult appreciating what she can do by herself. If adults do need to interrupt, they apologize. Infants who have been in respectful relationships and have been allowed to play freely do not need to be amused. Such infants have long attention spans for tasks they set for themselves. They are learning to learn. They are taking the initiative in doing what they want and getting what they want. They are learning to cope. The baby will let the educarer know when she is tired, hungry, sleepy, uncomfortable, needing reassurance, contact or comfort. It is the infant's capacities for independent play and need for sleep that allow an educarer the time to give uninterrupted attention and care to one infant at a time, while the rest of the group is engaged.

4. Freedom to explore and interact with other infants

Infants need freedom to explore and to freely choose activities that enhance their physical, mental and emotional development. Pleasure in the process of exploration and skill acquisition is self-reinforcing. The baby is empowered and begins to feel capable of tackling problems alone, rather than constantly expecting an adult to do it for him. In infant group care, RIE advocates that no more than four infants in similar stages of development be placed together, so they can explore more freely. This provides an environment where babies are safer from a more active and mobile older infant or toddler and where equipment is more appropriate for them and better scaled to their size. Infants grouped in similar stages are able to have more positive and more responsive care from their primary, familiar caregiver and are able to have more of a feeling of security and happiness. An older infant or toddler should only be brought in for a visit when the caregiver has the time to closely supervise and give affirmative guidance, rather than spending her time guarding the infant or saying "No" to the older one. Mixed age groups can work well for those above the age of 30 months or so, but to put a three-month-old with a one-year-old is unsafe. There is a high risk that the baby will be frightened or hurt by the curious toddler, whose judgment is not yet developed, but whose interest in the infant is high. RIE advocates that, from as early as four to five months of age, children benefit and learn from each other. Gentleness can be taught and reinforced by modeling gentleness. Young infants who are just becoming mobile learn to recognize one another and explore by looking and touching. When they are mobile, they are aware of one another and either approach or maneuver around one another as they creep from place to place. Social learning takes place as toddlers play together and learn how to solve conflicts, with an educarer available for safety and selective intervention.

5. Active participation of the infant in all caring activities

RIE encourages the involvement of children in all care activities to allow them to become active participants rather than passive recipients. As mentioned earlier, the classic case that Gerber cites for this is the process of diapering (Gerber 2000, pp.37–8). Because an infant's diaper is changed thousands of times and it needs to be done one-on-one, this is the perfect opportunity to develop a bond in the context of a reciprocal, respectful relationship. In practice, the educarer, whether parent or other adult, alerts the infant by speaking his name before touching. After a response, the educarer holds out her arms to show the infant what to expect, waits again for a response, then touches the child gently, and picks him up. The adult carries the very young infant in a way that supports the head and neck and tells him what to expect next – that he will get a clean diaper. A respectful relationship between the adult and each infant can be built, especially in caregiving activities in which the infant is allowed to cooperate to the extent of his abilities. Caregiving times are special times to build a respectful relationship between the adult and each infant. Because an infant's reaction time is slower, the carer allows "tarry time" (see Glossary) (Suskind 1985, pp.1 and 7), so that the infant is not rushed to understand and respond. The amount and quality of active participation changes as the infant matures and as the educarer notices what the child can do, and allows more and more participation.

6. Sensitive observation of the child in order to understand her needs

Sensitive observation is necessary to build the foundation of a respectful relationship. It is also necessary to foster the "authenticity" of a child. RIE supports educarers in learning to observe the child and develop their own capacity to guide, using their judgment to know when it is better to give no guidance, or just a little. The goal for RIE classes is to understand a child's needs and feelings. Each infant is treated as an individual and the adult tries to understand the baby's cues, to see the infant as a unique person and to respond appropriately. The child's self-initiation is valued and knowing when not to intervene is as important as knowing when to intervene. Observation is an art that allows the adult to perceive better the wants and needs of the child, and is used by the adult to help build a reciprocal relationship. Observation of the child also demands some self-awareness on the part of the observing adult. For example, the adult does not automatically feed a fussy baby, even if she herself is feeling hungry, but takes time first to try to ascertain the cause of the fussiness. If the toddler takes away a toy from another infant, and the other infant does not protest but rather seems pleased with the interest and interaction, the adult does not try to impose her values on young children who have not progressed to that cognitive level. Because babies learn what they experience, the educarer is careful not to use aggression to stop aggression in babies. Since adults also have needs and wants, the adult takes the responsibility for making these clear to the baby and, without rushing, takes care of those needs in a way which helps the baby to find life predictable and to take other people into account. For instance, if the educarer needs to go to the toilet, she tells the baby that she is leaving for a little while, that she will be back shortly and then, even if the child cries, she goes away and comes back as she has promised. By experiencing consistency, the infant learns, over time, to predict behavior and to trust that her carer will return soon. She will therefore be less anxious when the carer leaves briefly in the future. Modeling sensitive observation with the baby makes it easier for the baby to learn to observe and be sensitive to others, having experienced it herself.

7. Consistency and clearly defined limits and expectations in order to develop discipline

Infants thrive in a predictable environment. Consistency on the part of the adult makes the environment more predictable. Clearly defined limits for infants mean that the adults have to first consider and clearly define those limits for themselves. Expectations for infants need to be grounded in the knowledge of their growing capabilities. Human infants are born less physically mature than other mammals; they do not have the ability to stand upon birth, for instance, as a foal does. It would take a gestation period of approximately two years for a human infant to be equivalent in motor development to that of many other newborn mammals. The conjecture is that the large brain size in human infants precludes the pelvic expansion of the human mother, thus making birth after nine months impossible. Therefore, human infants are still physically developing out of the uterus, and inner drives for motor development occupy much of their attention. Only at around one year of age do infants turn their attention outside themselves (Eliot 1999, p.8).

Summary and conclusion

Accurate information about infant development is essential when setting realistic expectations that allow full use of the infant's capacities to make decisions and moral judgments based on her physiological capabilities. The learning activities, or "curriculum," which RIE promotes is based on a foundation of establishing a respectful relationship between the infant and a primary person, plus a few other significant adults who form a stable part of the baby's life. Within the relationship, RIE encourages the adult to become acquainted with the non-verbal infant through sensitive observation of the child's cues, and to offer both security and freedom to the infant within the relationship. RIE advocates setting appropriate limits for behavior while allowing the child to express his negative feelings as well as his positive ones, with the adult accepting the child whether he is happy, sad, or angry. It is important throughout all of the activities of everyday life that the educarer provides for the infant's self-initiated activity. One of the joys that makes an educarer's life interesting and rewarding is the challenge of a real, genuine relationship with an infant as he develops self-awareness and new competencies.

Chapter 4

Using the RIE Approach in a Family Day Care Home

Catherine Coughlan

...the educarer trusts the infants' abilities to initiate their own activities, choose from available objects, and work on their own projects without interruption.

Magda Gerber

Why RIE?

In 1986, after being a high school teacher for many years, I became interested in learning about early childhood education. Not having any children of my own, all I knew about taking care of children was based on occasional weekend visits from my nephews. My experience with the day care system was even more limited.

I enrolled in a variety of early childhood education courses and visited as many day care centers and family day care homes as I could (family day care providers in the US are equivalent to childminders in the UK). Observing the centers and homes first-hand gave me an understanding of the wide variety of approaches to day care and also helped me develop an ongoing relationship with a large number of day care providers and center-based staff whose advice and support would prove to be invaluable.

During a visit to a community agency that operated several day care programs, I shared my growing interest in infant/toddler care with the director. She described the work of Magda Gerber and gave me the RIE video, *Seeing Infants with New Eyes* (RIE 1984). While watching Magda on the video, I felt a strong connection with her because her approach to being with infants resonated with the way I had learned to be with high school students – encouraging their active participation in the learning process and respecting their individual pace and personalities.

Shortly after viewing the video, I attended a presentation Magda gave at Stanford University. I was more convinced than ever that I wanted to study with her and was delighted to find that RIE offered certificated training in southern California (see Chapter 7). I signed up and headed for Los Angeles to begin my introduction to RIE on a day that turned out to be my birthday in more ways than one.

By the time I began the RIE training I had already decided to become a family day care provider. Taking care of a small group of young children in my home appealed to me. Initially, I thought I would provide care for children of varying ages under three. After a few days of experiencing the RIE approach, it became apparent to me that starting with a small group of very young infants close in age – about three to four months old – would be a much more beneficial experience for them and for me. Before elaborating on the rationale for this type of age grouping, let me explain a few things about family day care in the US.

Family day care in the US

Since regulatory authority over family day care homes in the US is under the jurisdiction of state governments rather than that of national government, establishing and maintaining a family day care home varies considerably from state to state. In California where I was a family day care provider, the regulations are determined by the state legislature (with the governor's approval), codified by the state Department of Social Services, and monitored by staff in the district offices of the Department's Community Care Licensing Division.

In California there are two types of family day care homes. A license for *small* family day care permits one provider to care for a maximum of eight children; no more than two of the children may be under two years old, and two of the children must be six years or older. If only children under two years old are being cared for, a maximum of four children is allowed. A license for a *large* family day care home permits the care of a maximum of 14 children but no more than four of the children may be under two years old. In addition, two providers are required in a large family day care home.

After applying for a family day care license, the prospective provider is visited by a representative from Community Care Licensing. An inspection of the home must take place before a license can be granted. The main focus of the inspection is to verify compliance with the state's health and safety requirements. To receive a license for a large family day care home a fire marshal's clearance is also required. Additional regulations imposed by the city and/or county in which a large family day care home is located may also apply. Current licensing regulations require follow-up inspections of the home every three years. Unannounced inspections must take place whenever a complaint is made to Community Care Licensing.

The prospective provider must also verify that all adults (18 and over) residing in the home and all adults assisting in the day care home have proof of a current tuberculosis clearance and have submitted fingerprints for a criminal record and child abuse index check.

Since 1992 California regulations require family day care providers to complete 15 hours of training in pediatric CPR, pediatric first aid, prevention of infectious diseases, and prevention of childhood injuries. No other training is mandated for licensure. In order to be licensed for a large family day care home a provider must have at least one year of experience as a regulated small family day care home provider or have been an administrator of a licensed day care center.

Some providers are exempt from getting a license. These include: providers caring only for relatives, providers caring for children from one family in addition to the provider's own children, care being provided between parents when no fee is charged, and parents sharing the cost of care by a provider in the parents' home.

Compared to nannies and day care centers, family day care is usually a less expensive (but not necessarily an inexpensive) way for parents or guardians to provide care for their children. Several government subsidies for day care are available for families. California Work Opportunity and Responsibility to Kids (CalWORKS) is a welfare program that gives financial aid and services to California families making the transition from welfare to work. The CalWORKS Child Care Program provides day care subsidies to eligible families. The Child Development Block Grant (CDBG) provides day care subsidies for eligible low-income families who were never on welfare. Subsidies for day care are also available to low-income families through the Alternative Payment Program (APP). Because funding from both CDBG and APP is limited, applicants may be placed on a waiting list. The amount of the day care subsidy from all of the above programs varies depending upon such factors as family size and income level. There may be no cost to the family or the family may be assessed a fee based on a state regulated payment schedule. Subsidies are sent directly to the providers, but families choose the day care setting for their children. The setting may be a day care center or a family day care home (either licensed or exempt from licensing).

In the US there is a great deal of variety among family day care providers. Some are mothers who decide to stay at home with their own children while taking care of others' children. Some started out this way and continued doing it after their own children passed the day care age. Some started later in life when their adult children were no longer living at home. Some providers care for mixed ages while others concentrate on infants/toddlers (newborns to two-year-olds), pre-schoolers (three to five-year-olds), or school-age children only. Some base their approach solely on their own parenting experiences, while others combine this experience with classes or workshops in early childhood education.

For some providers, the day care income is supplemental; for others, it's the main source of income. Most are independent providers, but some are part of a network of providers hired by agencies providing day care in the community. An example of the latter is the Neighborhood Child Care Program offered by the Family Service Agency of San Mateo County in California. The agency, a private, non-profit organization, employs family day care providers as well as operating several day care centers. The agency handles most of the administrative tasks, including enrolling children in the family day care homes. In addition to receiving a salary and benefits, the providers are supervised by a child development specialist and they receive ongoing training in early childhood education.

The status of family day care in the US during the time I was a provider (1987–1992) was not very high. This was reflected primarily in the income level for day care workers in general. Family day care associations at the local, state and national levels have attempted to counteract the prevalent notion that "anyone can take care of children." The National Association for Family Child Care has a voluntary accreditation program that was designed to promote and recognize high quality, professional family day care. Also, Worthy Wage campaigns throughout the country led by volunteer activists continue to address the compensation issue by staging events to publicize the valuable, or should I say the invaluable, services provided by both in-home and center-based day care workers.

Being safe and free

One of the first things I learned during the RIE training was how important it is for infants to have a physically safe environment. In her book, *Dear Parent: Caring for Infants with Respect*, Magda Gerber states: "I consider safety the prerequisite for implementing the RIE approach. By safety I mean an environment which is so totally safe that, even *without* any adult supervision, the infant or toddler would be totally safe" (Gerber 1998, p.157; her emphasis).

With this in mind, I used a family room where the infants could lie on a flannel sheet on a carpeted floor. Since the four infants were three to four months old and were not sharing the space with older children, this was a very safe place to be. As the infants grew older and were able to move about the room, everything added to the environment was safe for them to play with and explore.

Another basic principle of the RIE approach is allowing the infants freedom of movement. This means not restraining them in devices such as swings, bouncers and walkers. (Because of injuries and fatalities associated with the use of walkers, California law prohibits their use in all licensed day care settings.) Since infants learn through their bodies, they need to be unrestrained so they can learn to move and move to learn. Each infant has his or her own timetable when different movement skills such as rolling over, crawling, sitting up and walking will be attained.

Equally important are all the movements the infants make in between these milestones that prepare them for the next one. Infants thrive physically and emotionally when not rushed to achieve these milestones. Having an infant develop trust in his or her body is facilitated by caregivers who also trust the infant's process. Putting simple crawling/climbing structures in the play area as the infants progress through different stages of motor development gives them an opportunity to follow their natural desire to move their bodies in new and challenging ways. Feeling both safe and free enables infants to be relaxed and energized at the same time. A great deal of learning takes place when infants are simultaneously peaceful and playful.

Uninterrupted playtime

A key component of the RIE approach is allowing infants to have uninterrupted playtime. When the infants in my day care home were not eating, sleeping or being diapered, they always had uninterrupted time to play. It is amazing how engaged infants can be when given both the space and the time to discover things on their own. Rather than interfering with an infant's play to teach them how to make toys work, it is important in the learning process to let the infant experiment. For example, several empty plastic cups of different sizes offer countless opportunities for experimentation. I often wonder if in attempting to teach infants how to play, adults foster short attention spans. Infants engaged in the discovery process have long attention spans.

The most intriguing play objects for infants are also the simplest. RIE recommends open-ended toys that can be fully manipulated by the infant. Many of these toys can be found in one's kitchen cabinets – plastic funnels, strainers, cups, bowls, containers, lids, lightweight metal bowls and frozen fruit juice tops. Other toys such as balls of differing textures and sizes and soft blocks can be purchased at low cost. Placing a few of these objects near the infants gives them a choice of which ones to play with – another important component of play. Open-ended toys have endless possibilities for experimentation because there is more than one way to play with them and more than one thing to learn from them. As the infants grow older these same toys continue to engage their curious minds because they discover new ways to play with them.

A great deal of my time during the day was spent sitting near the infants observing them. As I watched them play, I learned to appreciate their unique ways of doing things – how they moved, how they manipulated things, how they interacted with each other, how they coped with challenges – the list is endless. Sometimes I would make a comment such as "I see you are very interested in rolling that ball." RIE recommends being specific while making such comments to infants. By letting the infants know precisely what they have done, the caregiver is sending the message that she/he is really paying attention. It also contributes to the infants' language development because what they are doing is being verbalized by the caregiver. Commenting on play also requires sensitive observation: to know when to say something – and when not to say something – because it would interrupt the infant's learning process. Paying attention to the infant's cues is essential. Magda Gerber's fundamental advice is "Observe more and do less."

The value of caregiving times

Each mealtime and diaper change provides a built-in opportunity to be fully present with an infant. Instead of seeing these as chores that need to be done, the RIE approach encourages taking advantage of these one-on-one interactions to develop a respectful relationship between caregiver and infant.

Because of their different ages, the infants in my day care were rarely awake at the same time. This allowed me to take care of each infant's feeding and diapering without rushing through them. When an infant was hungry, I would tell her I was warming her bottle. When the bottle was ready, I would offer it to her, letting her choose when and how much to drink. All of these things tell her I care not only that she gets fed, but I also want to feed her in a way that respects her as a person. The sense of security an infant develops when treated in this way helps her develop trust in herself and others.

The same is true for diaper changing. I would tell the infant that it was time to change his diaper. It might sound something like "I can see that you are having fun with that bowl and now it's time to change your diaper." I would wait for the infant's response. Sometimes just the sound of my voice was enough to draw interest away from the play object. Sometimes it might take a few moments for the infant to drop it. Then I would tell him that I was going to pick him up and take him to the changing table. The diapering would then become a mutual give-and-take as I let the infant know what was going to happen. I would ask for his help and wait for it. Usually it did not take very long. If he wanted to play, we played for a while. The uncanny thing about diapering in this way is that it does not take that much time to change the diaper. The benefit is the cooperative relationship that develops during the diapering. Both infant and caregiver are learning to read each other's cues in working together to get a task accomplished. Rather than quickly getting the job done or forcing an infant to have a diaper change in an unpleasant way, the caregiver is utilizing this valuable time to lay a foundation for mutual respect during all types of interactions.

Infants who experience this type of responsive caregiving during feeding and diapering are quite independent during their playtime. Because they receive focused, responsive attention during caregiving, the infants do not need to be entertained. They are content and eager to explore their environment on their own. This ongoing cycle of intimacy during care-giving and self-direction during play allows the infants to thrive from both experiences. In a group care setting it also creates a much more peaceful environment than one where the provider is constantly trying to deal with crying babies whose needs are never quite fully met.

As daunting as the group care of infants might seem, the very fact that all the children were about the same age helped make caring for them easier. From the beginning, the infants were fascinated with one another (see Figure 4.1). Sometimes they would just look at another child – as only an infant can; sometimes they would reach out to touch the other child. I also discovered that placing an infant on the floor next to another infant helped facilitate transitions from a departing parent or from me after a caregiving activity. It was quite remarkable seeing how interesting and/or comforting one infant's presence was to another.

Figure 4.1 From the beginning the infants were fascinated with one another

The infants' families

Even though the infants spent a great deal of time with me (up to ten hours a day), their families would always be the most important people in their lives. During our first meeting the parents told me what they wanted for their infants, and I explained the RIE approach to them. This meeting always took place outside of day care hours so we could focus on the parents' needs and concerns. Interested parents would then return for a visit during day care hours to observe.

Once their infants were enrolled, the parents were always welcome to drop by during the day. I also let them know that if they called and heard the recording on my message machine they were not to panic; it meant I was taking care of one of the infants and would call them back as soon as possible. The parents were very receptive to this practice.

When the parents arrived to pick up their infants, we always chatted about their child's day. They also read the charts I prepared detailing information about what and when the infant ate and/or drank, when the infant slept, and when diaper changes were made. Each daily report included something special about the infant's day. It might be about an interaction the infant had with another infant or about something the infant discovered or particularly enjoyed that day. If an infant had any difficulties with eating or sleeping or showed any signs of not feeling well, I discussed these directly with the parents. If anything of a serious nature occurred, I called a parent immediately to let them know what was happening.

The program grows

When the children were two years old, two newcomers joined the group. The new children were a little younger but their developmental needs were similar to those of the original group. Even though my license did not require having an assistant, I felt it would be beneficial to do so because of the increased size of the group. I hired a part-time assistant whom I trained in the RIE approach. He was an enormous help in providing care for the six children, and I felt it was an added plus that he was a young man.

When the six children were three years old, I applied for and received a large family day care license because two of the children now had newborn siblings, and their parents wanted them to be in the same day care home. I hired two part-time assistants to provide a pre-school program for the older children. We gradually phased into enrolling more pre-schoolers to allow the six children and their new caregivers to become accustomed to one another.

One of the bedrooms was converted into a playroom for the two infants. I decided against enrolling more infants because I had the added responsibility of supervising my new assistants while providing care for the infants.

My day changed somewhat in that I now took care of the two infants until my RIE-trained assistant assumed this responsibility in the middle of the afternoon. I spent the rest of the afternoon with the pre-schoolers. This worked out well because I was able to maintain the close relationship I had with the children who had been in my care, and it gave me the opportunity to get to know the pre-schoolers who were newly enrolled.

When the second set of infants became toddlers, another toddler joined the group. Providing care for three toddlers was quite manageable because their eating and sleeping routines were fairly well established and, being toddlers, they were much more independent than infants.

As my fourth year in day care began, there were up to 12 children enrolled: three one-year-olds and up to nine pre-school-age children ranging in age from three to four years.

Rationale for separate age groups

I am often asked why I kept the different age groups separated. Usually the added comment is that the younger children can learn so much from the older children. While this is true, I found several factors influenced my decision. Safety is a major issue. Day care environments suitable for one age group are usually not safe for a different age group, especially where infants, toddlers and pre-schoolers are concerned. I also noticed that when, on rare occasions, the age groups were together the older children tended to dominate the play. For instance, the toddlers usually imitated the older children's play rather than initiating their own play. I also noticed a difference in rhythm – each developmental stage seems to have its own tempo. Mixing tempos seemed to detract from rather than enhance the quality of the children's play.

Occasionally the pre-schoolers – one or two at a time – would use the infant play area when the infants were asleep in another bedroom. They seemed to like re-exploring the things they had played with as infants. One child particularly enjoyed using the infant play structures – almost on a daily basis. He was three years old when he started coming to my home. He had cerebral palsy and using his strong arms, he would pull his body up through a large plastic cube with openings on six sides. He was so proud of himself when he was able to use his legs to help push his body through the top of the cube. His beaming smile is something I will never forget.

Outdoor activities

From early infancy the children spent a great deal of time outdoors. There seems to be something magical about being outside in the fresh air – watching leaves blowing in the wind, seeing a cat climbing the fence, feeling the breeze on one's face, hearing a bird's song or a dog's bark. These gifts from nature cost nothing and are invaluable sources of enjoyment and learning.

As the infants grew older and became toddlers and pre-schoolers, wheeled toys and climbing structures were added to foster the children's development throughout the different stages of their growth. Water and sand play were enhanced by using everyday household items such as funnels, buckets and scoopers. Kitchen items purchased in secondhand stores and hardware stores provided some of the best toys to use in the yard. The children enjoyed planting seeds and tending to the garden. They loved making chalk drawings on the concrete. When they were finished they seemed to have as much fun scrubbing away their drawings with water and brushes as they had creating them. In fact, cleaning things always seemed to be a favorite activity. I remember once they asked if they could wash my car (it really needed it). It was quite a sight to see the pre-schoolers with their buckets and brushes and soap suds galore reaching as high as they could to get the car clean.

The pre-schoolers regularly went to one of two local parks or explored the neighborhood on foot or in wagons especially designed for young children. The wagons seated six children with each child having his or her own seat. The children sat two-by-two facing the front. The seats were on a graduated slant enabling each child to have an unobstructed view. It was easy to push the wagons because they were well engineered. (Although RIE does not advocate using wagons because they restrict the children's freedom of movement, I used the wagons as a safe way to take several children at a time on field trips.)

During these trips the children saw all types of construction work going on. One time, after observing city workers digging up the street to replace the water pipeline, they went into the yard and began replicating what they had seen using plastic pipes and shovels – part of their collection of toys that was always available to them.

Often they would act out things they had done with their parents. Once they connected the deck chairs together with water hoses to make a "train." One child directed the activity and acted as the conductor, "selling tickets" made of scraps of paper to other children as they "boarded" the train. Another time they asked for my help in hoisting a water hose over the branch of a tree. I didn't ask them why because I had learned that they were always up to something ingenious, and facilitating their play was much more important, and productive, than questioning their motives. After adjusting the hose to their specifications, I observed that the children had asked me to put the hose over the tree branch so they could lift up a wheeled toy (designed like a car) to do a "lube and oil" job on it. They were "mechanics" for most of the afternoon.

When the pre-schoolers were on one of their excursions, the toddlers played in the family room and yard. Sometimes the toddlers and I would take trips around the neighborhood too. We would visit the local bakery and get fresh whole grain bread to eat on the way. Then we would stop by the grocery store and get some fruit – bananas were a real favorite.

All these activities were quite simple and did not cost a lot of money. (The wagons, however, were a major expense but were worth every penny.) Sometimes activities originated from the daily flow of life in a household. The children seemed particularly pleased to be able to help with household tasks such as wiping the table and folding laundry (both of which were initiated by the children). These many different types of activities enhanced the children's physical, social, mental and emotional development as well as contributing to their use of language.

In reference to language development, a particularly interesting thing happened with one of the toddlers who understood and spoke no English. He had been coming to day care for only about a week when, as usual, the children were engaged in water play outside in the yard. After I said that I had forgotten to get the sponges, he immediately went into the playroom, opened the cabinet where the sponges were kept and brought them out to us. His response is an example of why RIE advocates talking to children in a normal, conversational way rather than teaching isolated words.

Challenges

I think state legislators need to be proactive in ensuring that licensing regulations not only provide for basic health and safety provisions, but also make family day care settings ones in which children can thrive. In my opinion, group sizes approved by licensing regulations are too large and the ratios of children to provider, especially for infants, are too high. I kept group sizes down and ratios low, but this increased operating expenses and ultimately contributed to my closing the day care. This raises the issue of the need for more broad-based subsidies for day care. Even in years with surplus budgets, such subsidies are not considered. In lean years, existing subsidy levels fall short of the need.

The vast majority of families require full-time care for their infants. In the five years I provided day care in my home, I only received a few inquiries about shorter hours for infant care. Even though the RIE approach can and does provide a valuable service in promoting respectful, responsive interactions between caregivers and infants, I feel there needs to be a better balance between the amount of time spent by infants in day care and the time they spend with their families. This again raises a complex economic issue. How can single-parent families reduce their workday and still manage financially? How can low-income families, many of whom hold down several jobs, threaten their livelihood any further? It would seem paid family leave is an option families could take advantage of, but where will the money come from?

A major difficulty I experienced was recruiting and retaining qualified assistants. This was particularly problematic for family day care because of the status issue mentioned above. It took several months for me to find my first assistant, but fortunately he was referred by another family day care provider. He was very competent and remained until the day care was closed. Subsequent hires were much more difficult to find and to keep, but I was able to hire some assistants who were excellent. One became pregnant, and started her own family day care home after her baby was born. Another became ill and was unable to continue working in my day care home. Another was a high school student in a work study program who was very willing to be trained and became quite competent. It seems in large family day care homes, family member teams (mother/daughter, wife/husband or other combinations of family members) are more successful in keeping their day care homes open.

A big part of the recruitment and retention problem is the low wages that can be offered to caregivers. Even if day care fees are high, by the time all expenses are factored in, wages remain quite low. It was a challenge for me as well because I wanted to pay my assistants a much better salary than they were getting. I was also unable to provide them with any medical benefits. Attracting applicants with degrees or specialized training in early childhood education was out of the question because of the compensation issue. A major reason I decided to close my day care was because I, too, was making an inadequate income. Improving compensation is a significant part of any solution to the recruitment and retention problem.

Conclusion

Based on my experience, I feel a family day care home is an ideal setting for applying the RIE approach to infant day care. Working with a small group of infants within the intimacy of a home enables a provider to create the safe and free environment that infants need. It also gives the infants continuity in the caregiving they receive because their provider remains the same – an important component of the RIE approach.

Many times throughout the five years I took care of children in my home, I felt deep gratitude to Magda Gerber and Emmi Pikler for their contributions to the field of child development. RIE taught me how to be with infants in a way that I had not known before being introduced to Gerber and Pikler's work. I believe it was the insights gained from RIE that helped the children thrive in a peaceful environment that was both responsive to their needs and respectful of their capabilities (see Figures 4.2 and 4.3).

Figure 4.2 An environment which is "safe and free"

Figure 4.3 An infant who is "peaceful and playful"

Chapter 5

Creating Quality Infant Group Care Programs

Polly Elam

Infancy is a vulnerable stage of development, therefore it's not enough that babies receive good care, the care must be excellent.

Magda Gerber 1985

This statement has been a driving force in my professional career for the past 22 years and, at times, has seemed like an impossible goal. As a director for a very large public funded child care program that included infants as young as six weeks, I was at a loss how to create "excellent care for infants." My professional background had prepared me to work with children as young as three; infant group care was not well established in the US and there was very limited information on how to create quality programs for them. (In the US the term "infants/toddlers" covers newborns to two-year-olds, while "pre-schoolers" means children from three to five years old.)

My studies with Magda Gerber and my experiences with the staff, children and families in my programs have provided me with insights into the essential components of "excellent" care. It not only helped me with my work in my own programs, but has also enabled me to provide training and support to other child care programs.

The first step to creating quality infant care is to understand the true essence of "relationship-based" philosophy. This term is often used to describe the RIE approach and in recent years has been adopted by many programs in early education. While they use the term freely, there are some who do not fully understand the concept. They still want to define and control the relationship. This means they "have" a relationship with the child rather than they are "in" a relationship. There is a very subtle but vital difference in the meanings.

Relationship-based philosophy, as Magda Gerber defines it, is one based on mutual trust and respect for each individual. It is demonstrated by caring and interacting with the child in a way that communicates, "I want to know and understand who you are and I'm prepared to help you understand and know who I am."

Many adults who work with infants believe they already understand infants and know what is best for them. This may be true in the broadest sense, but one never really knows the individual child until one is in a relationship as Gerber defines it.

We encourage caregivers to approach each child with a sense of "wonder" rather than a sense of "knowing." This creates a paradigm shift and broadens their perspective, allowing a deeper understanding of the child. From this level of awareness, I have observed adult/child relationships evolve into a respectful connection where the caregiver assumes the role of guardian, allowing natural development to emerge in the child. The need to control the child is lessened. It's interesting to note that when a caregiver becomes skilled in this approach with children, it also enables her to create a more respectful relationship with adults.

Herein lies the key to implementing the RIE approach in group care programs. If we can help caregivers see infants in the way that Magda Gerber has taught us to see them, then their ability to create high quality care will follow. However, there are other contributing factors to consider.

A commitment to the relationship with infants goes hand in hand with a commitment to the family. This can sometimes be a challenge but one we must embrace if we are to create "excellent" care. Often in public funded programs, the family fits into specific categories that qualify them to participate. This is where a breakdown in personal identification and integrity can begin. Managers often see the family within the context of this qualifying category and, more importantly, the families begin to see themselves in this way too.

RIE encourages managers to focus more on each individual family and strive to understand their unique situation. They must be interested in and value each family's "story." Further, management must work to keep the caregiving staff focused on the same aspect of the family relationship. When this happens, everyone can work together to ensure each child has the opportunity to develop to his or her full potential. This vision of the family will become the catalyst for a strong partnership based on mutual integrity and respect.

Groups and ratios

To further support the development of the relationship between the child and the adult, a quality group care program must be organized into small groups of three to four infants with one primary caregiver for a major portion of the day. This person is responsible for all aspects of the care including diapering, bathing, toileting, feeding and documenting growth and development. When the primary caregiver is not available, there should be a secondary caregiver who is consistently assigned to this particular group. It is essential that the two carers share a mutual respect for each other and the work. They should also have the opportunity to communicate on a daily basis in order to share insights and observations of the children in the group. The ratio of one adult to three to four infants recommended by RIE is consistent with California state and federal regulations. Although each state in the US has its own regulations most require the same ratio of adults to children.

If necessary, two small groups of three to four children each can be combined in one room but each group should have their own primary care-giver. In this arrangement, it is possible for the secondary staff member to provide support to either caregiver but the number of adults in the room during the major portion of the day should be limited to two. While it may seem strange to limit the number of caregivers in the room, it is often dis-tracting and over-stimulating for the children to have too many adults in the environment. (The National Day Care Standards operating in England and regulated by Ofsted require ratios of 1:3 for under 2s, 1:4 for 2 year olds and 1:8 for 3–7 year olds (DfES 2003b].) As far as RIE-influenced provision is concerned there are generally six to eight infants in a group with two adults. Usually, there is another adult available to give the staff a break and to provide support such as cleaning up and so on. However, more than two adults in the room at any one time is discouraged. I encourage staff to ensure one person is low down or sitting on the floor with the children while the other may be changing a diaper or doing something similar. I refer to this as reducing the "giants" in the room.

I have worked with programs where it was not possible to have smaller rooms for each group of children, but we were successful in providing the same type of environment by rearranging furniture to establish boundaries within a room (see Figures 5.1 and 5.2).

Figure 5.1 Christina Heileg playroom, Konstanz, Germany

Figure 5.2 Out on the deck at Cottage Infant Toddler Center, Santa Barbara, California

Continuity

Another essential element found in a RIE-influenced program is continuity of care. This type of care involves a commitment from the primary caregiver to remain with the group until they reach the age of three, longer if possible. Typically, the group stays together in the same playroom with the same caregivers, changing the environment, equipment and materials as the children grow and develop.

This can be a difficult plan where there is a high turnover of staff. But many of the programs I work with report a reduction in staff turnover after they implement continuity of care. They attribute this to the close connection the caregiver feels toward her group of children (see Figure 5.3).

Amy Weaver, owner of Daily Discoveries Child Development Center in Maryland, has created an effective incentive program, funded by parents, with the expressed goal to support continuity of care. They ask the infant teachers to make a commitment to a group of children from infancy to age three. At the end of that commitment, the teachers receive a significant monetary bonus. Parents believe the program has provided more stability and better care for the young ones.

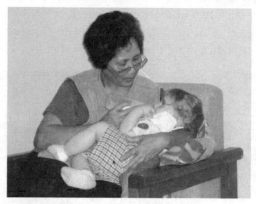

Figure 5.3 The close connection between caregiver and child

Caregiving routines

Sensitive, caregiving routines are another major factor in developing secure, respectful adult/child relationships. They should be planned and organized in a way that supports this development. This means time should be given so that the adult will feel less pressured.

Diapering should be a pleasant time for both the adult and the child. When adults expect that the child can and will be a willing participant, it becomes an opportunity for developing a close relationship. There are times when the child might fuss or wiggle around and then the sensitive adult slows down and allows the child some time to adjust and help with the task.

The child's sense of self begins to emerge during this kind of caring routine. During meaningful interactions, the child may attempt to engage the adult in a playful exchange, similar to teasing. This can become an opportunity for the child to learn to negotiate if the adult joins in the play. Adults who are focused on the task rather than the relationship feel rushed and often miss the child's attempt to engage them.

The same opportunity for building relationships exists in feeding and mealtimes. While most programs require infants to be held when they are given their bottles, many do not provide the same closeness when the child is older. I often see children propped in a high chair and left with finger food on the tray. They are expected to eat alone while the caregiver is busy elsewhere. Mealtime is not valued as an opportunity to develop relationships and social skills.

A small table where the child can sit without being propped up is the ideal setting to support this stage of development. Interactions during the meals are enjoyable and help to develop language. In the beginning, a caregiver may choose to feed and focus on one child at the table while the others play nearby, but later, two or more children can come to the table together. When the caregiver remains at the table, actively engaged and responsive, the experience becomes more than just getting fed (see Figure 5.4).

Figure 5.4 Mealtimes should be more than just being fed

When the mealtime is pleasant the child feels secure and competent. This feeling of competency is demonstrated in many ways – using the spoon to serve themselves from the serving bowl, wiping up spills or pouring their own milk from a small pitcher.

When visitors see our pre-toddlers pouring their own milk, they are often surprised. They want to know how we taught them to do that. We don't teach pre-toddlers to pour their own milk; we allow them to pour it because they can.

The group care environment should reflect the age, development and interests of the children in the group and it should be physically safe to reduce the limitations and support the child's feelings of competence and independence. With careful planning, children will feel free to explore and play, allowing the primary caregiver time for individual caregiving routines with another child.

It is also important to recognize that adults spend a major portion of their day in this environment. Careful attention should be given to the comfort of the adults as they give care. RIE discourages the use of rocking chairs because generally staff sit in them when they hold the babies to give them their bottles or feed them. The gentle rocking often puts the child in an altered state of consciousness and likewise the adult. We feel that during the feeding they both should be alert, especially the adult. When the child falls asleep in the arms without having finished the bottle or food, the caregiver, thinking the baby is full and sleepy, moves him quietly to bed. Often the baby awakens earlier and the caregiver, misreading the cues, perceives the baby is fussy and tries to get him to sleep again. We want the caregiver to understand and look for cues that indicate the child feels satiated and only move the baby to the bed when he is sleepy. We also encourage caregivers to allow the child to "self-sooth" and settle themselves for sleeping, of course, with our close monitoring. Also, we believe that rockers in the environment are dangerous for children who are creeping around (fingers under the rockers) or pulling up to stand.

However, we do believe the adult must have a comfortable chair that is ergonomically correct to support them while holding and feeding the infant. The environment must be pleasant for both the adults and the children.

Curriculum and learning

At this point, one might ask how curriculum and learning fit into this program where the emphasis is on relationships and caregiving routines. In a RIE-influenced program, relationships and caregiving *are* the curriculum. We believe learning takes place in every aspect of the child's day.

We do recognize that infants are born into the world with the innate drive to figure out how it all works. As the child develops motor skills and becomes more active, it is important that plans are carefully made to support their interests and abilities. Therefore, we encourage caregivers to use their understanding of the child, gained through their daily observations, to plan for the child. They create environments with interesting objects and materials, allowing the children to explore freely on their own. The emphasis is on discovery rather than teaching. The caregiver becomes the facilitator and the resource, and is available if the child needs her. Otherwise, she or he sits and observes and gains additional insights to support expansion of the curriculum when the child is ready.

We have learned that infants and toddlers tend to focus more on their play when one caregiver, at least, is seated on the floor where the children are exploring. The caregiver can use this time to make written observations, yet be available if a child needs support or simply wants to be near the adult.

Toddlers are more active than infants but are not yet pre-schoolers. Many programs make the common mistake of creating a toddler environment and curriculum similar to the pre-school program. While it appears toddlers are ready to learn through group activities, this is not always true. In an effort to control the active toddler who is not ready to work in groups, an inexperienced caregiver is often drawn into "entertaining" the children. When a child does not participate, she sees the child as difficult and might take inappropriate measures to discipline the child. This can often weaken the adult/child relationship because the toddler, at the critical stage of "autonomy vs shame and doubt," feels shame or anger, and the child is labeled difficult in the caregiver's mind.

In his "Eight stages of psychosocial development", Erik Erikson (1965) defines this period as one where the child begins to develop self-control and self-confidence and actively moves toward autonomy and a certain level of independence. The implications for the adult are to create an environment where the child can explore freely and have many choices for exploration and discovery.

Toddlerhood is a unique period and the emerging development of the toddler should receive the same considerations as when planning for infants or the pre-school child. The environment, activities and materials should foster the development of autonomy and support the toddler's natural curiosity and discovery.

While toddlers do need to "check-in" with the adults from time to time, they seldom need the adult to teach them how to play and explore. Rather, they need the adult to be physically and emotionally available to them – a resource and champion for this marvelous phase of life.

The staff team

This brings me to another essential component in a high quality infant group care program – a dedicated and knowledgeable staff. It is not enough to have caregivers who "love" children. It is vital that caregivers understand how infants and toddlers develop and have realistic expectations for their behaviors. Caregivers must maintain a curiosity and enthusiasm for life and have the capacity to share that joy with the children.

Caregivers must be emotionally healthy and be open to diversity, accepting of each family's unique culture and lifestyle. Likewise, caregivers must be committed to their own professional growth and development.

And finally, quality infant group care programs happen when the leadership has demonstrated a commitment to quality. I add "demonstrated" here because it is not enough to *say* we are committed, our commitment must be shown through our actions – through the policies we write and strategies, including financial support, which we develop for implementing them.

But most of all, leadership and management must recognize that creating and retaining high quality caregivers is their responsibility. If we are to maintain high quality programs where infants are not damaged, we must ensure we have a strong workforce of caregivers who are respected and valued as a profession. We must ensure they have physically safe and emotionally nurturing environments in which to work. They must have time to plan and be together in order to develop an understanding of each other, the children and their families and to build trusting work relationships. Caregivers must have opportunities for professional growth and development and receive wages and benefits commensurate with the responsibilities of the work they do.

"It's not enough that our babies receive good care, it must be excellent" (Gerber 1985). Our families need it, our caregivers want it, and our children deserve it.

Chapter 6

RIE Parent–Infant Guidance Classes

Elizabeth Memel and Lee Fernandez

You don't have to teach. You don't have to buy more gadgets. You don't have to do anything. Both of you can just exist and enjoy the developing relationship between you.

Magda Gerber

RIE's collaborative model of human development

Infancy is an active learning phase and the RIE model of parent–infant guidance classes presents possibilities for building respectful relationships between child and adult from birth, thus supporting healthy, secure attachments (see Glossary). RIE works on the premise that learners across the life span take a more active role in the educational process if they learn in relationships with each other. Those who teach infant caregivers attempt to engage students actively in their education, and involving parents of very young children in the educational arena is a widely accepted strategy in the US. A collaborative learning model can be more effective than the limited "professional as expert" model and, indeed, that model has been questioned in complex Western societies as our understanding of diversity and difference has increased. The collaborative triad formed over time by infant, parent and RIE facilitator is one based on sensitivity and trust where mutual sharing of information occurs and where parents and educators can be resources for each other.

The experience of becoming a parent activates two sets of deeply embedded unconscious memories: the memory of how one was parented and the memories of how it felt to be a child – as we wittingly or unwittingly do unto others what was done to us. With its greater access to childhood memories, early parenthood can capitalize on the capacity to empathize with the young child and support individuation more readily. RIE's preventive approach seeks to help establish patterns of healthy self-regulation that may evolve when the adults caring for their baby are given the chance to see that child as the unique human being she is. When the child is seen as a competent human being, as the weekly demonstration in a RIE class evidences, respect for her part in co-determining her development is greatly enhanced. Weekly support groups provide the context for developing this kind of understanding and vision as the infant's point of view gets taken more and more into the parents' perspective. Then slowly the principles of the RIE philosophy may become part of parents' awareness, their thinking and actions. Eventually, when they truly become part of the parent, the principles can serve as parents' own inner guidelines.

> There is no question that, thanks to learning the RIE approach to caregiving, I am a very different person than I would have been. I'll even go so far as to say it has changed my life. Most of my friends agree with me that we all said "I'll never grow up and be like my parents" – and yet we do…parenthood has forced me to face some crucial issues in my life… I didn't know that learning to be a better parent was going to be my first step toward such an incredible period of personal growth! (Mother at RIE class evaluation, 2001)

Respect for infants is not the only guiding principle in RIE's approach. Parents bring socio-cultural and ethnic diversity to groups and provide the opportunity to experience and respect differences in existing parental practices. Seeing the differences and similarities in cultural, familial, and parenting styles can give a broader perspective to one's own parenting. During these formative stages, parents are in the best position to learn from others, especially from models that provide personal interaction and kinship in the context of group support. With regular attendance and participation, there is no end to the benefits a well-organized support group can provide for parents/carers and their infants (see Glossary).

RIE parent–infant classes as a learning process

RIE's goal is to help raise "authentic" (see Glossary) infants who are competent, focused, peaceful, involved, cheerful, cooperative, resourceful, initiating, confident, aware, secure, attentive, curious, exploring, interested, and inner-directed. Parent–infant guidance classes are the heart of RIE. "In our program parents are guided to learn how to observe, understand, respect and enjoy the individuality of their own and other infants" (Gerber 1997, p.71). Here is where we see the philosophy come to life and where we see what happens when babies are trusted to be independent learners.

The RIE parent–infant guidance class philosophy (taken from a leaflet for parents) states:

> We believe that infancy is a crucial time of life when basic patterns of coping, living and learning are set. Parenthood is a most important, challenging and difficult vocation. From the beginning, parents could be better prepared to make parenting easier and more rewarding. The abundance of publications and activities for infants produces controversy, confusion and pressure for parents. To quote mothers: "Whom do I trust?"–"Too much advice"–"Too little help"–"Nobody really shows me how to apply it to my baby."

To meet these needs, the RIE program is based on demonstration. In an infant-oriented environment, children are encouraged to become attentive, active, exploring persons who are self-rewarded by development arising from an effortless and dynamic unity of their sensory-motor skills. Parent–infant classes are held weekly and continue, ideally, for the first two years of an infant's life. In small groups of similar age/stage of development, the infant is given space to move in, appropriate objects to manipulate and other babies to watch and with whom to interact. The group facilitator demonstrates special methods of selective intervention (see Glossary) that allow the child to reveal himself, to make his own choices and to evolve his own style as he learns to become self-reliant. Infant education in the RIE program is based on a problem-solving approach that has a lifelong effect.

Infants are observed individually and in groups by their mothers, fathers and/or caregivers who are participating and involved in discussions on related topics. Parents find their relationships with infants more rewarding as they discover:

- what to realistically "expect" of the infant at any given stage of development
- when to intervene in an infant's activities, and even more important, when not to
- how to synchronize infants' changing needs and parents' wants and needs
- how to observe, understand, respect and enjoy the individuality and competencies of each infant.

One of the hardest parental tasks is to try to understand the baby's feelings and needs, to interpret these as best he or she can and to respond in a way that is appropriate. Since the infant cannot talk, adults (both parents and caregivers) may be unable to determine exactly what it is the baby wants or needs. Feeling helpless, inadequate and becoming frustrated, adult caregivers sometimes project their own needs and feelings onto the baby, or may interrupt the baby because they cannot imagine the communication or activities of the child could possibly be more important.

> Babies from birth on try to communicate how they feel. If your attitude is, "I cannot know automatically what you need, please tell me", then the baby will learn to give you cues, and a dialogue will develop. If, on the other hand, a mother superimposes her interpretation of the baby's problems, the infant will *un*learn to expect appropriate responses to her needs, and learn to accept what mother offers. This is the difference between being understood and misunderstood. Being understood creates security, trust and confidence. Being misunderstood creates doubt both in yourself and in the problem. (Gerber 1998, p.63)

In RIE parent–infant guidance classes parents are assisted by the facilitator to become more attentive, sensitive observers of their children. Sensitive observation of babies enables parents and caregivers to make fewer, more selective, more effective interventions in their child's activities. In this way a wait-and-see attitude develops: looking for cues from the baby, slowing down, allowing the infant to take more initiative and to solve problems using her own coping devices. Magda Gerber suggests adults "observe more and do less" (Gerber 1998, p.63). The parent then becomes less active and therefore less burdened and frustrated, and the child becomes more active and therefore freer and with fuller access to self-expression. The infant, vulnerable as she is in many ways, is not helpless. The RIE philosophy validates infants as competent human beings and their competence is observable through the experiential process of learning in the classes.

The RIE approach shows that observation leads to understanding and understanding builds respect. When the parent provides a secure base (see Glossary) from which an infant's exploration can take place, the child develops trust – in self and in others. Basic trust evolves from being allowed to explore safely, in the protective context of parental acceptance, not only the beckoning physical environment but also the wide range of feelings that are developing. Responsiveness to a child's signals on an emotional level, quiet availability and facilitation of the striving for independence supports the child's autonomous functioning and helps him achieve a sense of his own competence. This respectful observation promotes skillful, non-intrusive interventions.

> Once you learn how to observe, how to pay full attention, your relationship with other people, grown ups included, will also change. You give them a gift by telling them with your attentive behavior, "You are worth my interest and full attention." Every human being likes to be listened to, to get genuine attention, to feel understood, accepted, approved of and appreciated. (Gerber 1998, pp.64–5)

Framework for RIE parent–infant guidance classes

Classes may be held in spaces as small as the living room of a modest house or as large as an exercise studio. The play area must be made safe for infants and toddlers in the usual ways – electrical outlets covered, doors hooked open or shut, danger areas gated or fenced off, no electrical cords or table lamps. An environment that is interesting and developmentally challenging to babies cannot be absolutely, unconditionally safe, but the body control and synchronization that babies develop through naturally repetitive and unrestricted movements adds an inner safety factor. Parents and caregivers must make their own determination of the acceptable balance between challenge and safety in the play area for infants and toddlers, both at home and at child care centers. Magda Gerber's vision has always challenged parents' resourcefulness and encouraged infants' autonomy by emphasizing the establishment of one safe space at home to allow for solitary, uninterrupted play every day for infants of all ages and stages.

What is the ideal environment for baby's exploratory play? There should be surfaces of different textures and heights to be crawled, climbed, walked, and rolled over, under, around and through or to be sat on. Perhaps there is a hardwood or linoleum floor, a soft rug that doesn't shed, a mattress and pillow soft area, maybe an empty inflatable wading pool, low platforms, a low ramp or slide, cardboard cartons of varying sizes, a hollow wooden cube for tunneling or climbing, low wooden stairs, hard bolster pillows, open-sided cubes or low shelving for storage. Choose only a few of these furnishings, as the most important part of the environment is space to allow babies to move freely.

A variety of "toys" are available where infants and toddlers can reach, choose, touch, finger, grasp, push, pull, mouth, chew, hold, hug or carry them. Many are common household objects chosen because they are lightweight, washable, safe (no lead paint or toxic chemicals, no small parts or sharp protrusions), and non-breakable (no brittle plastic). Simple toys lend themselves to inventive and open-ended activities. These toys and objects have multiple possibilities for manipulation and use. More complicated toys may have limited, or only one use. Toys that require the infant to be active while the toy is passive are the truly creative toys. Instead of being passively entertained, the baby is an active player.

Observation of infant aged nine months*

A nine-month-old in a RIE class in Silverlake, California, was observed playing with contented concentration for 19 minutes with a cotton scarf. He did everything you could think of with that cloth: shook it, squeezed it, flipped it, transferred it from hand to hand, pushed it, pulled it, put it on his foot, hand, head, in his mouth, rubbed himself with it, threw it away and fetched it back, scrubbed the floor and wall with it, sat on it, lay down on it, played peek-a-boo with it. The scarf is truly an active-player toy with endless possibilities.

---

*All infant observations have been undertaken and recorded by Lee Fernandez.

The outside space can be on a patio, deck, balcony, or lawn. Space might include: soft grass, trees (no poisonous plants), clean sand for toddlers, water, wood, cement, outdoor carpet, stone surfaces of different levels, ramps and low stairs. Slides and climbers, which might be a bit more challenging, can be added as the infants' developing competence allows them to be included safely.

When the scene is set and the space is ready, a few toys are put out inviting baby to reach and touch. Most of the toys are neatly arranged in their familiar place on open shelves or in open-sided storage crates or bins. For the youngest floor-bound babies, a clean sheet spread over a thick rug or mat, peaked cotton scarves, a few whiffle balls (plastic with small finger-sized holes throughout), a partially inflated beach ball, and assorted teething toys are all that are needed.

Parent–infant guidance staff consist ideally of a parent-educator/facilitator (who facilitates discussion and answers questions) and a "demonstrator" (who is responsible for the children, sits on the floor with them and demonstrates, rather than talks about, RIE methods). The former facilitates parent interaction and discussion. The latter is necessary to take responsibility for the group of children, because if parents interact only with their own infants, there is little opportunity for them to learn from behavior modeling. When parents must take sole responsibility for their own child they are less able to be observant and are more likely to anticipate behavior and intervene unnecessarily in their child's activities. They will also not be able to participate fully in discussions. However, the presence of the facilitator makes observation of other parent–infant interactions possible. Feedback about interactional behavior is more effective in changing parent behavior than when parent discussion alone is used, although both methods are effective. A skilled parent-educator may be asked to take responsibility for the children during discussion time since it is possible for one staff person to handle both of these tasks.

Enter five or six babies at a fairly similar stage of development, with their moms, dads or, perhaps, their grandparents or carers. Classes for the youngest infants last for an hour and a half, although toddlers may come for a two hour class. Parents are asked to spend the first half of class time observing their child and the other children. In the second half, after snacks for infants who are able to move to a sitting position on their own (discussed below), there is time for discussion and questions. A staff member is in charge of the children at all times, giving parents more freedom to observe or participate in discussion. Adults may place the youngest babies on their backs on their own blanket or quilt (it will smell and feel familiar in this strange room). Their carers will probably sit quite close, at baby's feet, facing each other around the sheet or rug. The parent-educator/facilitator has very little contact with the infants in the early months of classes, so the models for parents are primarily each other. However, parents are also in the process of building trust in the facilitator. Later, when the infants become more mobile, a demonstrator needs to be active on the floor, available to intervene if necessary. Occasionally, crawling babies create infant-infant interactions that could pose a safety hazard, but they provide two of RIE's important lessons: deciding when to intervene and when not to intervene. Meanwhile, the facilitator has been intervening for the adult listeners during the sessions, weaving information into discussions and giving feedback that is based on the curriculum emerging from what the infants are experiencing and demonstrating at the time. At first (newborns to about four months) the primary carer (usually the mother) and baby form a unit that is almost inseparable. The RIE classes provide a place where a very gradual infant-initiated separation can begin. As the baby learns to move, he or she is free to leave the parent/carer, sitting on the floor along the edge of the space while able to return or check in with physical or eye contact at any time. Sometimes it is the separating parent who leaves the room for a short time – always telling the child first – and always returning. Older, mobile babies may first sit in their parent/carer's lap and then may be put down on the floor, as long as the infant's point of view is being regarded and considered by the adult. The baby may decide to stay close to her carer for a long time, touching her, watching, or playing nearby. Adults are encouraged to stay in one place for most of the class, as a safe base so their child can easily locate them whenever they are needed. The babies have complete freedom of movement and can interact with each other, any adults and the environment, with minimal restraint. A very gentle, non-rescuing intervention is used if a child becomes frustrated, upset, physically stuck, or seems about to hurt another child. Sometimes, just the adult getting close, or verbally reflecting the interaction, is all that is needed. Parents and babies are treated with complete respect: feelings are regarded as valid experiences and are acknowledged, not ignored, minimized or ridiculed. Rather than the adult swooping in to make everything all right, we wait to see if the baby will solve his own problem, offering the minimum amount of adult intervention or "help" necessary. Restraint in adult intervention has a purpose: to encourage infant problem-solving and self-reliance. We are giving the child the chance to do as much as he can do on his own – always being available if help is really needed or wanted. The extent of the help is determined by the situation, but if there is no danger, the child's power should not be usurped. This is central to the RIE philosophy of infant education and care. Essentially, babies explore and play while parents/carers and staff watch. Of course, the youngest infants are floor-bound and relatively immobile. However, the focus of attention is on the babies' "authentic" behavior – being and doing exactly what they can and want to do. Socialization begins as the child approaches one year, when a snack time is introduced, which the baby may choose to join or not. Initially, the snack may be offered picnic-style using a plastic tablecloth placed on the floor. Certain behaviors, such as sitting on a low stool and staying at the table while eating or drinking, are expected and the children begin to learn limits. Simultaneously, the parents see how to begin to introduce discipline through patient, predictable and consistent reinforcement and limit setting (see Chapter 2). Between 12 and 24 months, other behavior limits are consistently reinforced, such as not leaving the playroom or not hurting another child, not throwing objects other than balls, and so on.

The RIE philosophy and methods are demonstrated to parents more by the environment and the staff attitudes and presence with the children, than by theoretical explanations. A feeling of calmness, safety and trust makes it easier to be observant and attentive.

Observation of a one and a half hour parent–infant guidance class for five infants aged 9 to 12 months with their mothers and one demonstrator/educator and one visitor*

Erica (ten-month-old girl): just walking, her mom says. Mom sits nearby after putting her on the center rug; Erica looks at us, cries out and crawls to mom and sits.

Simon (ten-month-old boy): mom sits along edge of rug space nearer the wall, puts him on floor in front of her; he looks at us a moment, cries briefly (hears baby in hall crying), crawls across rug toward wood platform, along the way picks up a plastic fish, and hits it on an empty plastic soda bottle. Erica making lots of happy sounds, crawls a bit away from her mom, crowing.

George (ten-month-old boy): mom sits away from rug, puts him on his back. He looks at demonstrator and at mom. Erica crawls toward George, George looks at Erica and at his mom. He wiggles his hands and looks at Erica. Erica sits and holds a small toy. She looks at George and crawls toward her mom. Simon watches and plays with a metal pan lid. Erica gets next to her mom, holds her shirt and sucks on the toy she has been carrying. Simon kneels, holds pan lid and looks at Erica. Erica stands next to her mom, looks at Simon, gets down and crawls close to the rug.

Paul (eleven-month-old boy): mom sits near the rug holding Paul; then he stands close to his mom. She walks across the rug to put away her glasses and comes back. George is sitting on his mom's leg. Paul returns to his mom's lap. Erica crawls back to her mom, holds her mom's foot and chews on a toy. Simon is playing with a metal pan lid, picking it up and putting it down. He crawls across the rug, stands up holding the edge of the plastic storage bin and pulls down the nesting toys that were on top. Paul holds his mom's shirt as he sits between her legs. He looks distressed. Simon is intently pulling apart the nesting toys. Now he takes a tumbler and mouths it. George shows his mom a toy. Erica has been sitting near demonstrator. Erica crawls toward Paul who backs off slightly (demonstrator gets close). Erica squats and looks at Paul and Paul's mom.

Paul's mom says Paul has been cranky lately: discussion of teething. Erica sits on the rug mouthing a toy. Simon is nursing. Erica crawls over to Paul and his mom. Erica stands and offers a plastic cube to Paul. Paul holds his mom's shirt with one hand and takes the cube. He holds it. Erica takes the toy back. Erica crawls over to Paul's mom. Erica kicks a curler and it rolls away; she watches the curler. Erica crawls to her mom and gets in her lap.

Simon gets up on a cushion; his mom and the demonstrator are nearby. Simon squats. George is at the toy bin. He mouths a juice can lid and drops it: clink. He picks it up. He picks up a wooden car and drops it: clunk.

Julie (twelve-month-old girl) and mom enter. Julie is put on the floor, sitting. Demonstrator gets close as Erica comes close to Julie. Erica crawls close to her mom. Julie stays close to her mom, climbing into her lap to be held again. Simon is playing with a toy phone close to the demonstrator and now moves back to the pillows. Erica gets close to George's mom and holds her shirt as she stands and gets down. Erica goes back to her mom. Julie crawls away from her mom. Erica crawls away from her mom. Simon crawls back to his mom. Paul is nursing. George plays with a soda bottle on a wooden platform.

Paul moves away from his mom. He gets near Julie and her mom. Julie very gently reaches out and touches Paul, not poking, she's interested. Julie grabs her mom, holds her shirt and toy to mouth. Julie mouths Paul's cheek. Paul is accepting, not scared or anxious. Paul looks at his mom. George watches Paul and Julie. He looks for his mom, finds her and looks at her. Paul crawls to a doll near George. George moves his foot off the doll.

*The names of the children have been changed to ensure anonymity.

RIE and parents/carers

Parents are treated very gently. Certain expectations of the supportive environment need to be articulated as "ground rules" for adult interactions. Modeling the respectful approach, staff do not judge, directly admonish or blame parents. Parents may choose to use self-reflection and also may choose to share insights with the group without judgment or criticism imposed on one another. No one ever says: "Don't do that; you will damage your child" or "This is the right way to do it." The parent-educator brings parents' attention to the large and small changes in their child's abilities and competencies. Naturally, the parents are already in communication with their child and can often translate a child's need (by the tone of a cry for example) to the demonstrator. Noticing that they already have special knowledge about their child's needs is a positive reinforcement of parenting abilities.

As trust in the environment grows, most parents in the RIE setting are eventually able to relax and allow themselves to enjoy just being with their babies, delighting in their child's development and forming realistic expectations of behavior as they observe other children at the same or slightly different stages. Teaching parents to be attentive, accepting observers of their children rather than anxious, intrusive observers or absent non-observers can free them from some of their fears as to whether their child is growing optimally, and can relieve some of the guilt working parents may be feeling about long, daily separations.

However, during the first few months, as the demonstrator responds to the activities of the children, parents often have questions. Since the children are grouped by development and somewhat by age, mothers, fathers and carers have common concerns such as teething, sleeping problems, weaning and finding the appropriate balance when needing to get away from the stress and fatigue of constant care. Discussion of how each family deals with these concerns is encouraged at this stage. The parent-educator/facilitator also comments and gives reasons for trying one method of handling a problem rather than another. Always the emphasis is on the parent's need to make conscious choices, to examine why they make specific choices, and the necessity of doing what feels comfortable and right to the parent. A parent attempting to adopt a pedagogical method that is unfamiliar and not fully understood cannot help but give confused messages to a baby. It is better for both parent and infant if the parent does what feels natural and at the same time self-observes, becoming more conscious of her/his own behavior and trying to discover why a particular response or reaction feels right. It is also important for the facilitator to support this process in which parents become clearer about what they value or appreciate, and observe how the baby actually responds to their behavior.

Occasionally, there is a specific topic for the day's discussion. Usually, parents bring up their concerns, which are always of general interest. The babies' interactions and their changing development also spark topics and questions, providing an emergent "curriculum" for the class. The safety of the environment and the presence of the demonstrator inevitably build trust, encouraging parents to permit their infant or toddler maximum freedom of movement and discovery, thus allowing anxious or over-protective parents to see their child as more able and competent. As parents observe their child's trust in the demonstrator and the environment, their own trust is reinforced.

Observation of a parent–infant guidance class during a ten-month period from when the infants were about four weeks old until they were active babies

Newborns

Watching the parents of four-week-old babies: the mothers hover fairly constantly and are aware of every nuance of their baby's expression or movement. The babies can't change position much and parents stay very close, perched on back-supporting floor cushions. Each baby's expressions are minute and each mother is extremely attentive and reads a lot into every turn of a head or a long direct look, a groan or a sigh. Babies are frequently fed, held or doze off.

Three to four months old

At three to four months old, although there is still not much mobility, there is now such a special "beingness" to each baby. The person within the infant is starting to show itself to us. There is such intense concentration on fingers, on a scarf placed within sight and reach, or on another baby. Moms sit close, occasionally they feed or hold their baby, but they spend more time observing what the baby does. Babies are very aware of each other, looking and listening.

Six to seven months old

At six or seven months old a parent is willing to sit near; baby may move away a bit by wriggling or rolling. Baby is babbling and expressing a lot of different feelings and meanings. The parent has the baby's language down pat. "Oh, that's her hungry (or sleepy or 'look at me') cry." Mom can tell more from baby's sounds and movements and doesn't need to gaze so intently at her face to see what the baby's needs might be. The physical shape and size of the group expands as parents sit further back, allowing the babies more space to move; mothers are willing to physically separate themselves from their babies more of the time.

Ten months old

At ten months old baby and parent sit together at the edge of space and then, after a warming-in time (which varies considerably in length according to baby's mood and personality and the adult's signals), the baby leaves mom, ignores mom, and gets interested in toys, other babies or other adults. There are definite, frequent, physical returns or checking-in glances when the baby makes sure mom is where she is supposed to be (those refueling and security checks we read about: see Glossary). Parents or caregivers often go to the aid of their upset or stuck infant. The babies are so incredibly inventive. Anything you can imagine doing with the toys and objects or another baby's body, they manage to try.

As baby begins to walk, leaving and returning is a continuing saga. So many looks of triumph! The just walking baby is constantly on the move, abandoning the long intent explorations of objects of pre-walking days. There is a return to interest in investigating and manipulating of objects once walking has been achieved.

16 to 24 months old

As baby gets closer to talking, mom increasingly expects the baby to alert her to problems, rather than anticipating or decoding baby's expressions or gestures. The great day comes when the toddler realizes he can get an adult involved in a verbal dialogue. "What's dat?" (pointing again), "What's dat?" ad infinitum. The child can now capture and direct the adult's attention whenever and wherever he wants to. The power of words!

Parents/carers

The adults are also demonstrating communication, for during the second half of the class, parents, and sometimes caregivers, talk animatedly with each other about a variety of day-to-day problems. They are full of comments and questions, especially since the parent-educator has spent a good bit of time refocusing the group's attention on the babies during the first half of the class. Parents usually sit in one area as the babies go to and from another area. Refueling glances and returns for cuddling or just a touch continue, mostly if there has been an unsettling change or a bump.

As shown above, the whole picture for a family has changed during the experiential process of group sessions from infancy to toddlerhood. First baby was stationary and floor-bound and the parent moved and anticipated and responded. Later the parent/carer stays put and the baby is the mover, going to and fro, getting and asking for what she wants and needs. The baby's needs have changed. The transformation for parents is as dramatic as it is for baby. From the bonded, attached all-comforting parent, she becomes the parent who must let go and allow the child first to move away and come back, and then to express intense feelings of independence or the contradictory and inexplicably instantaneous need to hold on and not let go. The child's desire to move away gradually strengthens, though when the mother leaves (to use the bathroom or get a fresh diaper from the bag on the shelf in the next room), the child's anxiety may be dramatically demonstrated by desperate crying.

The child's feelings of competence seem to be connected to her parents and caregivers in two ways:

1. There must be willingness to let the baby explore and become independent, and support for the baby's attempts to separate or stay close. Adults can help the baby through upset and failure by expecting but not pushing future success.

2. The parent or primary caregiver has to be there, be the touchstone, the permanent secure base, the safety net.

Parents and carers have to give three messages:

1. You can do it! It's OK with me that you move away and try out new things.

2. I'm here, right beside you, and it's OK with me if you choose to say close.

3. I'm not going to leave you; I'll tell you if I go out, and I'll come back.

An expert parent-educator/facilitator can really encourage animated and honest discussion between parents, even when their viewpoints differ. This is particularly valuable in ensuring the inclusion of families and children from diverse communities or who have special educational or physical needs. The key seems to be valuing all contributions and validating them as a reflection of each individual's experience. Exchanging ideas and ways of dealing with the same problem gives parents a chance to consider the possibility of alternative solutions. Parents of very young children need to share their anxieties, upsets and uncertainties, and who can better share a parent's joy and delight in their child's latest triumph than a parent with a child at the same developmental stage?

At the same time, RIE teaches parents to be respectful of their own needs and feelings. Parents are encouraged to think and talk about what feels comfortable for them and for their babies. We discuss where these feelings come from: our own forgotten infancy, parenting we observed or experienced as older children or as siblings, what we have heard and read, and our socio-cultural traditions and values. We encourage parents to parent by choice, as they feel, to be sincere and authentic, and know why what they do is right for them and for their baby. We encourage thinking and mindful decision-making about parenting, rather than just reacting or letting whatever happens happen. No one can be totally consistent, that wouldn't even be helpful to babies or parents, but it is possible to be more consistent and more content when we are doing what feels right to us. In RIE parent–infant guidance classes, parents become the experts on their own baby.

RIE parent–infant guidance classes for vulnerable children and their families

Intervention must highlight the strengths that families have, rather than underscoring the weaknesses. RIE's non-deficit model features empowerment as a process of change, over time, for parents of young children from any section of society. There are occasions in the US when a private or public authority will direct families with infants or toddlers to enroll in a parent education course because of either developmental or environmental risk to children. In addition, when authorities offer support groups at no cost to a community, families may be engaged who might otherwise not be able to choose involvement in beneficial programs. RIE parent–infant classes are not usually subsidized and parents commonly have to pay a fee. Although the organization is non-profit-making, the charge is higher than most impoverished families can afford.

A government-funded parent education series of six RIE classes was offered in southern California in early 2003. Funding came from taxes on cigarette purchases and all supported programs were expected to foster school readiness for new born to five-year-old children. Administered by the California Children and Families Commission (see Glossary), the three areas emphasized throughout the state are: early child care provision, child caregiver training and parent education. All costs of the RIE short series were met by public monies so that any family choosing to participate could do so at no cost if space was available. Thus, parents living in impoverished socio-economic circumstances wanting to learn about infant or toddler caregiving had the opportunity to attend. Since the RIE model of parent education limits class size to six to eight participants, families were accepted on a first-come, first-served basis. There were three consecutive Saturday sessions consisting of two classes each, so working parents were not excluded. One session was for crawling infants, from 11.30am to 1.00pm since they usually nap in the mornings and afternoons, and the other was for toddlers, 10.30am to 12.00 noon, so they finished in time for one longer midday nap. Adult participants included lone carers, both male and female, as well as two-parent families. The families were primarily Caucasian, most from lower socio-economic income groups, primarily educated to high school level and with several working mothers. The program will be repeated and, it is hoped, extended.

A further example of the provision of parent–infant classes occurs in Los Angeles City College. As an added resource on campus, the college has periodically offered free RIE parent–infant classes on a short-term enrichment basis. Both public and private funding made it possible to conduct two groups on six consecutive Saturdays for young children with working parents. A small staff of two college instructors and two aides set up the environment in a demonstration classroom and facilitated small groups of a maximum of eight families. Participating parents are sometimes the same students enrolled in the child development college class, who wish to apply the knowledge in a hands-on experiential learning environment. Other families are from the neighborhoods surrounding the campus. The budget allows for book purchases, so all families receive a copy of *Dear Parent* (Gerber 1998). Evaluation forms reveal how parents/carers experience the classes. One mother of an eight-month-old, with a toddler in the household as well, responded that she learned from "letting the kids solve their own problems…to use their intelligence to figure out what the toy does." She liked observing how her baby discovered another toy because it allowed her to "be independent and not always turn to me for help." She found that "living is easier because now I have time to do more things around the house and let them play in a clear and safe environment." Another parent whose toddler was 17 months old felt her attitude about parenting changed a lot by seeing that there was not a right or wrong way to play with the toys provided. "Helps children explore without intervention" and "I let my son be more independent" were her comments at the end of the series. When one parent allowed her child more freedom and stopped interfering, "always trying to teach all the time," she noticed her child's behavior "became more relaxed and not always looking for approval." Finally, a two-year-old's mother is behaving differently "because now I pay attention to my daughter's needs, since I understand more of her attitude. I learned that by sitting here and just observing my daughter. I pay attention to all the things that she does."

RIE parent–infant guidance classes as a learning tool for early years students

At an urban community college that awards Associate of Arts (AA) degrees for its two-year program, child development students have gained knowledge of the RIE philosophy over many years of course offerings on the subject of early childhood. In order to enrich the Infancy Studies course curriculum, multiple observations of the RIE parent–infant class model has been a required assignment. This experience presents the opportunity to develop a much deeper understanding of the RIE approach, which goes far beyond the college classroom text book learning, instructor lectures, or even videos. The collaborative learning experience of the families/students involved, based on demonstration, is primarily observational and experiential. Infants and toddlers developing "authentically" demonstrate the potential growth of autonomy as it is allowed to evolve in the playroom environment. College students are observing and taking notes for class assignments, and later large and small group discussions regarding new knowledge and implementation. The facilitator/instructor demonstrates respect for the authority and role of the parents while functioning as a resource for the college students and young children. Dialogues and discussions may be summarized by the facilitator, who offers key learning points and clarifies concepts. Expression of alternative viewpoints is encouraged and so adults learn the value of conflict when generating multiple perspectives. The small group work builds relationships that foster such learning. As they act and react in groups, students gain new information while discovering their own unique identity and human potential. Feedback from recent students describes what they learned from first-hand observation of infants, toddlers and parents:

- "Infants develop self-confidence when left to play. They are keen observers and good listeners."

- "A six-month-old was inner-directed, content with her mother fully present while the child self-entertained autonomously for nearly an hour!"

- "I could see that locomotion is helping develop other areas, such as socializing and communicating."

Reciprocity, a key feature of collaboration, is the influential dynamic learned between people in all our programs. The child and the adult influence each other's growth, and changing attitudes and behaviors continue as a dynamic, lifelong process.

Conclusion

As we have outlined above, parent education in a facilitated discussion format can be effectively combined with observation of infants by parents, interaction between parent and child, and interaction between infants. Through this interaction and observation, parents discover a lot about their child and about themselves. Interaction between parent and child can be both child and parent initiated if the parent is responsive, if the child is free to move and if the parent predictably stays in one place for long periods so that the child can find the parent again. There will also be many natural encounters between infants if adults do not interfere. However, when babies are in close proximity, an adult needs to be very near to anticipate and gently prevent a baby from accidentally hurting another. The essentials for this learning experience are: small groups (six to eight mothers, fathers or other carers and infants), a long, unhurried time (once a week for one and a half to two hours), a carefully prepared, safe space, a trained (see Chapter 7) parent-educator/facilitator and demonstrator, and a relaxed, sharing atmosphere (see Figure 6.1). Within this context the child can be truly valued just as he or she is. And the parent can be valued as well. Parents see the weekly gathering of families as a very special opportunity for peaceful checking-in on their lives and relationships. Many find support for their "authentic" expression via mutual sharing of concerns in the safe space where there's nothing to do. Rather, it is a time to be, to connect with others and their own baby, especially for those returning with their second or third child.

Figure 6.1 Carer feeding a baby in the supine position and showing total attention. The carer remains low so she is accessible to other babies. A crawling baby is able to be happily engrossed in her own pursuits while remaining close to the carer, touching her leg.

In the final analysis, in the RIE program, it is the infant who informs or teaches the RIE approach to infant caregiving. Parents are asked to come and spend one and a half to two hours a week observing their child's self-initiated exploratory behavior, from as young as two to three weeks of age up until about 26 months. Naturally, during the observation, time is spent "refueling" the relationship during the baby's numerous returns to the secure home base. But these separation or attachment choices are made mostly by the child, who feels growing trust in his or her own decisions. Of course, the parent determines if the cues from his or her child require a caregiving response of any kind – diapering, feeding, putting into a sleep space, and so on. The possibility exists for altered parental practices through a change in parents' knowledge or in parents' perception of children and the parenting role. The parents learn how competent and secure the child is becoming, week after week, and how the simple act of waiting to see what transpires before automatically responding supports this growing competence and "authentic" development. This is the "extra beat," as one parent defined it, or as another wrote, "I needed to slow down and wait for my child to show me the way."

Chapter 7

To Teach as Magda Taught
or
Mutual Respect and Trust:
The Role of the Mentor in RIE

Polly Elam

I now go to places and can see immediately if people understand the spirit of the approach even if they do things differently from the way I would.

Magda Gerber

When I began this project to define the RIE training program, I outlined a "how to" article, describing in detail the key issues of mentorship and supervising students. It began to read like many other books and resources available on the subject and didn't really reflect the essence of the RIE philosophy.

So I choose, instead, to describe my RIE experience with Magda Gerber, my mentor and friend. Hopefully, these short vignettes will give you some insights into her unique approach to mentoring others in this philosophy. While I took the opportunity to go through all the formal levels of the training, my understanding of the RIE philosophy happened in this mentor/mentee relationship. It is one of mutual respect and trust. I will admit that it was not always easy with her. She can be painfully honest and often pushed me beyond what I thought possible. But she also taught me that the struggle is the essence of learning.

She helped me understand and appreciate the world of infants and toddlers. But most of all, she helped me see, understand and appreciate the adults who work with them. And in the process, I have come to understand and appreciate my life's work and myself.

Give them what you want them to give the babies

One of the greatest challenges our students face when they have completed the RIE courses is sharing the philosophy with others. I recall how excited I was when I completed my RIE I training with Magda. She had given me a glimpse of infants through her eyes and I was eager to share my new vision with others. I "taught RIE" in 30 seconds to a new mom in the line at the grocery store, to harried parents in the airport, to new grandmas at the beauty salon, any place I could find an audience. Unfortunately, they were not always so happy to hear my lessons and my lectures fell on deaf ears.

At the time I was a Director of a large employer-sponsored child care center that included an infant care program. I was also a part-time instructor at a community college, similar to the further education colleges in the UK, so I often recruited my best students to work for me at the center. It was a bit easier to share the philosophy with them because we were already in a relationship of trust and on a journey to improve programs for children. They shared my interest and excitement in RIE and were open to trying this new approach. Together we began to implement the philosophy and make program improvements.

Unfortunately, I left that position shortly after my RIE training and relocated to another area within California. I assumed responsibility for a larger program with major problems. The new staff did not realize I was "wise and wonderful" and had come to make their work easier. They only knew I was making changes too quickly and they were not open to change. Keeping infants in wind-up swings all day kept them quiet and content. Why would anyone want to change that? Even the babies, who were accustomed to being restrained, resisted when I attempted to put them on the floor so they could move freely. Why should the staff try my new approach when it did not appear to work for them or the children?

One day, in utter frustration, I left work and went to spend the afternoon with Magda. As I began to pour out my heart to her, she asked if the staff were being abusive to the children. "No, not really," I replied. "They are just stubborn and won't listen to anything I have to say." I was convinced that I could make their working life much better if they would only cooperate.

Magda listened with empathy and I could sense that she felt my frustration. When I had finished sharing my dilemma, she said, "Polly, don't worry about the children right now. Go back and give the staff what you want them to give the babies." This was the day I learned my first lesson about sharing the philosophy.

"Give the adults what you want them to give the children." What an interesting concept!

It had never occurred to me that I should take time to understand the staff and their needs. Magda helped me realize that in order to help the staff, I must first show them respect, accept them and understand them. I had to give them time and involve them in the process of change. I had to listen more and teach less. I had to be in a relationship with them – a relationship based on trust. But first, I had to do the trusting. Later, they would begin to trust me, and from this relationship of mutual trust and respect, we could work together to improve programs for the infants.

I must confess it is much easier to give infants the time needed to develop and learn; there are times when I fall short of what I want to give adults. But I know this approach to sharing the philosophy with adults is effective. I continue to see changes in the staff and the program. They are learning and growing, but so am I.

Role-playing RIE

Through the years of sharing the RIE philosophy, I have become very interested in observing adults as they begin to understand and internalize the RIE approach in their own lives. I often think of my own experience as a RIE II student. When Magda encouraged me to enroll in this level of training I was excited, yet overwhelmed. I had come to admire Magda and wanted to learn everything she had to share.

The RIE II level is where students, who have a basic understanding of the philosophy, come to demonstrate their skills while working with the infants in parent–infant classes. It is somewhat similar to practice placements for trainee social workers or teachers.

I was assigned to work in a weekly class with parents and their infants in a parent and toddler (see Glossary) setting. I prepared the rooms with the objects and materials appropriate for my group of children. When parents arrived, they sat around the edges of the room with their infants during a "warming up" period. My particular group was early toddlers who stayed in their mothers' laps until they felt secure in the setting. Gradually, they would move out into the playroom and begin to explore with the materials and each other. My role was to observe and intervene when necessary to facilitate their exploration and interactions. Magda sat nearby with parents, answering their questions regarding the infants' development and experiences.

I can still recall how nervous I was during the first few weeks of my training. I wanted so much to be successful. I memorized all the lines I had heard Magda use in videos. "Do you want the yellow cup or the red cup? I see you both want that toy." I knew all the right moves – look into their eyes, approach slowly.

After each class, Magda and I would meet to review the events of the morning and discuss the children's behavior. Each week I waited for her to tell me that I was doing a great job. I wanted her to say I was succeeding. Instead, she asked me questions about myself. We talked about life experiences but very little about the children. I grew more frustrated with each passing week and finally decided that she was too kind to tell me I wasn't going to succeed at this level of training.

After much thought and soul-searching, I finally decided to give up. As I drove to the RIE center on the tenth week of my training, I practiced all the excuses I was going to use to quit the class. I felt like such a failure.

That morning with the parents and their infants was very peaceful, but I suspected Magda knew something was wrong with me. When we met later for our discussion, she began by asking me what was going on in my life. I tried to explain that I would have to drop out of the RIE II training, but she didn't seem to hear it. I gave her lots of excuses but she wouldn't accept them. Finally, I blurted out that I just wasn't "getting it". I wasn't learning anything from the experience and I felt like a failure.

In tears I said, "Magda, I am a competent person. I know how to be with children. I have learned all the RIE phrases and I can say them but they sound empty." I went on to explain that no matter how hard I tried, I could not be Magda Gerber; I had to be me.

She looked at me for what seemed hours and then smiled and said, "Polly, I think you have it. For the past ten weeks you have been role-playing RIE. I want you to be authentic so you can be in an authentic relationship with the children." It was then that I began to understand the personal content of our discussion during the past ten weeks. She wanted to know and understand me, but more, she wanted me to know and understand myself.

That day we agreed that I needed to continue RIE II training beyond the anticipated 12 weeks. While I laugh and tell people I flunked RIE II and had to repeat it, it was in those ten weeks that I learned an important lesson. Not only did I learn about myself, but I also learned a valuable lesson about helping other adults in their professional growth and development.

It's important to help them understand that who they are in the lives of children is more important than what they do. It's from a place of authenticity that we can accept and help others, both children and adults, become who they were meant to be. It's from this acceptance that people begin to trust. In a trusting relationship, real collaboration in the learning process is possible.

The messenger is also the message

Shortly after I became a RIE Associate, Magda gave me the biggest challenge of my professional career. Anita Garaway, Director of Great Pacific Child Development Centers, was requesting on-site training at her center in Ventura, California. I lived in Oxnard, only 15 minutes away. Magda asked me to work with the staff and offer the RIE I course. At first I declined, but Magda and Anita are the most persistent people I know, so I finally gave in.

Magda promised to be available to answer any of my questions or provide assistance when necessary. She also agreed to come to some of the classes and observe me and give me feedback.

I offered the course over ten weeks, visiting with Magda on a regular basis and sharing the discussion from each of the classes. She offered encouragement and gave me valid feedback and suggestions. The staff seemed to grasp the philosophy and were open to change.

I felt successful.

On the last night of the course, Magda was scheduled to visit, observe my teaching and meet the students. I prepared everything carefully, paying attention to each detail. I was well-organized with my lecture notes and my handouts. Magda sat quietly on the side and seemed to watch with pride. Everything was perfect. While I was nervous, I played the part of RIE I teacher as I had scripted it.

We ended the evening with a small party and I drove Magda back to the hotel. She chatted about each of the students and commended me for my work. Then she gave me another valuable lesson. "Polly, remember the messenger is also the message." I didn't quite understand what she meant by that statement, but I was too excited about my success and didn't want to dwell on that lesson at that moment.

In the following months as I discussed my teaching style with her, I began to understand the lesson of that night. In my attempt to make everything perfect for the class, I had made my presentation too rigid. I controlled the students' responses and questions because I lacked the confidence in my ability to truly share the philosophy in a way students would understand. I was attempting to teach the students about responsive relationships with infants, but failed to be responsive to my students. I was "teaching" the students, while trying to help them understand the concept of planning an environment where infants could explore and learn on their own. I talked too fast and moved information too quickly, while I was telling them to slow down for the babies.

As my mentor and teacher, Magda is clearly both the messenger and message. Her methods in helping me see the infants in a new way are consistent with the wisdom she shares about babies.

What do they want to know?

One of the most rewarding aspects of my RIE experience was the opportunity to travel with Magda. One such trip was to a local conference of the Southern California Association for the Education of Young Children in the Los Angeles area. I had accepted her invitation to drive her to present an afternoon workshop. I arrived at her home early to make sure we could have a leisurely drive there. I grew somewhat anxious as she took her time preparing for the trip, but soon we were on our way and the freeway traffic was light. We were enjoying the drive, chatting about the sights, when she suddenly asked, "What do the people want to know today?" I was shocked. "What do you mean, what do they want to know?" I asked. "I'm the driver, you are the speaker. What do you want to tell them?"

We laughed and teased each other a bit, but I soon realized she was very serious. She was off to present a workshop and was asking for my assistance. I quickly ran through some of my ideas for training, and suggested that we show a video clip on toddler exploration and have a discussion about it. She always travels with her "bag of knowledge" and I was confident she had just the right video for the discussion.

When we arrived at the conference site, I attempted to get her to the meeting room as quickly as possible so I could cue up the video. As is often the case, we kept meeting people who would stop her to chat, so we arrived late in the room. She settled herself at the front table while I fiddled with the VCR. I was having difficulty getting the machine to work and, when I did get it to work, I couldn't find the video clip I wanted to use.

After several minutes of waiting and in front of about 200 people, Magda asked, "Polly, what are you doing?" I was frustrated and somewhat annoyed. I responded in a low tone that only she could hear, "I'm learning a very valuable lesson." My lesson was to decline future invitations to drive her to workshops. She smiled and asked the group, "Then what shall we talk about while Polly learns her lesson?"

What followed then was incredible. The people began to ask questions and Magda entered into a dialogue that went on for two hours. Many issues were raised. They debated issues, shared insights and asked more questions. I witnessed real enthusiasm and understanding among the group. Magda challenged their thinking. She played devil's advocate when they offered solutions to problems, yet validated their experiences and thinking.

As I sat watching, I realized I was learning the real lesson of the day. While I was busy attempting to set the stage to "teach" them what I wanted to share, Magda was open and responsive to what they wanted to know. Needless to say, we didn't use the video that day.

While I have not developed the skill to present a workshop without some preparation, I find it most effective when I am open to what people want to know. I am often asked to conduct "as needed" training for programs. I make classroom observations in the morning and conduct workshops that evening, focusing on information appropriate for that particular group. It not only helps me with my training plan, but the morning spent in the rooms helps me to form relationships with the staff.

It is much easier for me to relate to the staff member's frustration with a child who bites when I have observed the numerous times she attempted to intervene. It is more effective for me to ask a well-placed question to stimulate problem-solving, when I witness, first hand, the stumbling blocks they are facing.

I have also come to recognize that Magda never really offered a workshop without preparation, either. I believe her preparation for sharing the philosophy came from the many years of being in relationships with infants and their parents. Her "knowing" comes from her keen and sensitive observation of children and adults. And while she teaches us that there are core values in the philosophy that never change, she encourages us to be responsive and fluid in a society that *is* changing. When we develop the capacity to be open to change while maintaining the integrity of the core values of RIE, we will have achieved the essence of the lessons she taught us.

Understand their vision of the child

"How they see the child is how the child will become. Understand their vision of the child and help them see yours." This was the lesson Magda taught me once while visiting my program. Several years had passed since moving to my new center, and we were making progress in understanding and implementing lessons from RIE.

A number of the staff had completed the RIE I course and I was eager to have Magda visit and witness her influence on my programs. After spending several hours visiting throughout the center, I found her silently observing two of my most challenging staff members. Later, when we talked, she described them as "RIE on the outside." They knew all the words, went through all the motions, but failed to internalize the philosophy. She validated my suspicion that they "did RIE" while I was around but went back to their old methods when I wasn't observing. I was expressing my frustration with these particular women, when she began to share several very positive and commendable qualities she had also observed in them. She offered no solution to my staff issues, but did leave me with hope. And, of course, she left me with those words – "Understand their vision of the child and help them see yours."

What a challenge!

In the days following the visit, I spent more time observing the two caregivers. We have observation windows in the center, so it made it easier for me to take a peek as I passed by. I watched for those positive qualities that Magda recognized in them. Soon I found myself sitting in the room, quietly observing them. At other times I visited with them in the staff room. Sometimes we chatted about the children in their groups, at other times we shared on a more personal note. I soon noticed they were stopping by the office more, asking for guidance on how to handle different issues.

Months later, during a noontime walk, I began to realize what was happening between me and these two staff members. I had just spent the morning in their room, observing a child who was experiencing some difficulties. While I finished the observation with lingering concerns for the child, I found I was at peace with the staff. As I continued my walk, I reflected on the events of the past months and all the changes that were happening.

During Magda's earlier visit, she had understood my vision of these two staff members. She validated my feelings and concerns, but left me with her positive insights and observations. I'm sure she must have picked up on inappropriate behaviors too, but she didn't focus on those. She helped me "see the staff with new eyes."

After that day, I began to follow her lead and do the same thing with the staff and the children. When they came to me with their frustrations about a particular child, I tried to understand and validate their feelings rather than criticizing their perspective. I would also try to point out a positive quality in the child, or throw in one of those "well-placed" questions to redirect their thinking. I noticed that they began to see and respond to the children with less frustration.

One day I realized we had come full circle in this process of influencing each other's vision. As I voiced my concerns about a challenging parent, one of the staff members said, "Polly, the way I see the parent is…" She went on to share her positive vision of the parent. I smiled inside and thought of Magda and what she had put in motion.

Magda, they hardly knew you – a lesson in relationships

Through the years of working with Magda, we developed a special friendship and shared many stories and insights. I was confident that no one else shared the same relationship, and kept many notes with the thought that I would, someday, write a book about our time together. The title of my book would be *Magda, They Hardly Knew You* because I believed I was the only person who truly knew her.

I have since learned that many associates at RIE feel they have a unique and special relationship with Magda too. I now recognize that she gave each of us what we needed in the way of friendship and understanding. This realization has helped me understand the essence of "relationships," which she so often spoke about.

Our relationship evolved through mutual experiences and understanding that grew from our sharing stories. She was always interested in my life and wanted to know and understand me. Likewise, she shared her experiences and was open to my many questions. She not only shared events of her life, but her feelings and thoughts. I never felt judged, but rather, always accepted and understood.

This lesson in relationships has helped me so much in my journey toward understanding others, and has helped me gain insights into anti-discriminatory practices.

Magda did not really address such matters in the RIE philosophy, but encouraged us to be open to others in a respectful way. In retrospect, I realize she was living the practice that everyone else was attempting to teach us in the many anti-bias curriculum lessons.

I find this lesson on relationships invaluable. Of course, I continue to be sensitive to social rules around culture, but I work harder at trying to understand others in the context of their culture and family lifestyle. I am eager to hear their "story" and I am open to sharing mine. I gain so much more from this practice. It's not only a great lesson in relationships, but also one in humanity.

In summary

Some years ago during a workshop in Santa Barbara, California, I shared the platform with Magda. The focus for the workshop was quality infant/

toddler programs in group settings. Most of the participants were my colleagues and students. We spent most of the day talking about caregiving routines and adult/child relationships. We questioned Magda and she challenged our thinking. We debated issues and again, she challenged our thinking. As the day went on, she kept asking the group if we believed that infants should be raised in group care. I finally responded that the reality was that infants *were* being raised in groups. "We want you to help us understand how to create the best group care possible for our infants." Magda looked at me in a way that only she could do and responded, "Polly, I don't deal with reality, you do. You figure out how to do it and you help them."

Those who know Magda recognize that while she understands, she is not limited by the realities of society. She always questions why our children cannot have the very best that society has to offer. And she challenges each of us to work toward that end.

Her challenge to me that day has become my life's work: to help people understand the needs of infants and toddlers and create the best child care programs possible. I believe this happens through comprehensive and responsive adult training programs.

In a time when society wants to do more to babies to stimulate their brains and make them develop faster, we must help society to recognize that the greater challenge is to help adults understand and be responsive to babies. Babies come into life with an innate drive to learn about and understand the world. Our work is to help the adults in the child's life, both parents and professionals, see the infant with new eyes.

Magda, with the support of many RIE associates and supporters, developed a professional training process that addresses three distinct levels. She also developed an approach to parent education through parent–infant classes. (This will be described at the end of this chapter.)

But I believe the most effective way to teach the RIE philosophy is grounded within the context of respectful, supportive and collaborative relationships with others who share your interest and curiosity. I must add that it also takes time to understand. Many come to RIE wanting to complete the course quickly, but to truly understand it takes time.

Magda says understanding RIE is like peeling an onion. I rather think of it as like eating an artichoke. At first it looks interesting. One might even be tempted to try the outer edges, but leave it because it's not that satisfying. Some continue to pull it apart out of curiosity until they get to the tender part. And just when they begin to enjoy it, they hit the "prickly part." It's those tiny stickers just above the heart. This is where most give up and believe they have had the best the artichoke has to offer. But those of us who have learned to love artichokes know that below the "prickly part" lies the very best part: the heart. As teachers and mentors, our role is to help the students stick around and get to the heart of RIE.

To summarize: the lessons I learned from Magda that influenced my approach to training are as follows:

1. Give the adult what you want them to give the babies. While this seems reasonable on the surface, it's not always easy. But it is essential. Through the years I have learned this lesson the hard way. There have been times when I wanted to say to difficult staff or students, "It's not about you, it's about the children." But it *is* about them. People who do not feel valued and respected have difficulty developing respectful relationships with babies and their families. It takes time for even the brightest person to fully understand the essential aspects of the philosophy. And while I get frustrated with their slow progress, I've come to understand that it takes as long as it takes. The important thing is to accept and respect individuals at their own level of understanding. And to communicate that acceptance and respect on a daily basis.

2. Create an environment where each adult feels emotionally safe, yet intellectually challenged to become all they were meant to be. Help them recognize that RIE is not about what they do, but about who they become in the lives of the infants. Recognize and acknowledge each person's gift to life.

3. Work hard to understand each person and help him or her understand themselves. Have the courage to give them honest feedback and challenge their thinking. Help them to understand, value and respect themselves so they don't have to play roles. Playing roles is too confusing to the children and the rest of the world.

4. Work hard to develop the skills and confidence it takes to share the philosophy with others. Create a style that is comfortable for you and is consistent with the message you want to get across to your students. Be authentic. Be open to other points of view, but remain faithful to the integrity of the core values of the philosophy.

5. Understand your students and be responsive to their issues and concerns. Find out what they want to know. Be prepared to adjust your course, lecture or workshop to meet their needs. Get them involved in solving their own challenges. Accept their solutions as

stepping-stones toward quality improvements. Each challenge is just another lesson waiting to be learned.

6. Understand their vision of the child and help them understand yours. Work on your vision of the adult. Find them doing something good and focus on it. You can't influence others until they trust you. And be prepared; they may have some lessons to teach you. Be open to them.

7. And last, but not least: you can't teach RIE to that harried mother in the grocery store line, but you can acknowledge that she has a hard job…and you can let her go in front of you in the line.

The RIE professional development courses

Methods for passing along the content of the RIE philosophy as well as its values and practices necessitate meaningful human contact based on respectful relationships. In California, RIE has developed two types of instruction. The first type is a class for parents who bring their infant once a week for observation and guidance in child rearing, usually until the toddler approaches two years of age (see Chapter 6).

The second type of instruction is for adults, generally in the early childhood profession (this is currently being re-framed so that it can be offered more widely).

It consists of a series of three courses – RIE I, II, III – with a specific curriculum and focus at each level. Completion of the course work can culminate in certification to teach either RIE parent–infant classes or RIE professional courses.

The basic course is also open to parents who want a more thorough background knowledge of infant development and care than is offered in the parent–infant classes. In the two later stages of professional preparation, mentoring of advanced students of RIE becomes an important part of the process. After attaining certification and becoming a RIE Associate, it is possible to continue the process of professional growth by joining an alliance of RIE certified teachers, which provides peer review and support.

RIE's three-part certification training is designed to enhance the skills and competencies of professionals who work in the field of infant care, who teach parent/infant classes, and teach infant development and care in colleges, universities or adult education programs.

RIE I Fundamentals: theory and observation

The introductory RIE I 60+ hours course includes an overview of the RIE philosophy: gross motor, fine motor, cognitive, and social-emotional development of the infant; designing the environment; planning the curriculum; issues in parenting, and visits to centers, family child care homes and special programs to learn to observe infants. It offers lectures, films and videos, experiential exercises, discussions, reading and writing assignments.

RIE II Practicum: demonstration and discussion

Graduates of RIE I may apply to enroll in this Practicum for a minimum of 12 weeks. While the RIE parent/infant teacher and parents relax, seated in a circle around the infants on the floor, the RIE II student, who is with the infants, demonstrates when and how to intervene and when not to intervene with the infants in a way that will optimize their development. A conference between the RIE II student and the teacher is scheduled immediately after the class to discuss the experience gained and the lessons learned.

RIE III Internship: supervised teaching and evaluation

Graduates of RIE II may apply for admission to the highly selective RIE III internship. RIE III interns are mentored to deepen and internalize RIE I fundamentals. Group and self-evaluation are included. A minimum of three iterations is required. It is also necessary to complete a project of value to the RIE organization. Until readiness to teach is attained, further training will be recommended. Certification is awarded when the intern achieves readiness to teach RIE parent/infant observation and guidance classes. Additional academic background, and the ability to teach adults, is required for certification to teach RIE I classes. On satisfactory completion of RIE I, II, and III, the student becomes a RIE Associate.

Membership of the alliance of RIE certified teachers

RIE associates who want to be authorized to teach RIE accredited classes are eligible to apply for membership of the RIE alliance. Here, peer review and support are offered. Teachers are expected to keep current on their dues and responsibilities annually. More experienced teachers of RIE parent/infant classes may be authorized to mentor RIE II students in their classes.

Chapter 8

Applicability of the Pikler/Gerber Approach in the UK Context

Sue Owen and Stephanie Petrie

Introduction

Emmi Pikler and Magda Gerber demonstrated respect for young children in their work spanning more than 50 years. As outlined in Chapter 1, they have shown that respectful care promotes optimal development and supports healthy attachment relationships. Their work was theorized and implemented in very different socio-economic, ethnic, cultural and political contexts. They cared for children of varied capabilities, with a range of physical and learning differences, living in both affluent and disadvantaged circumstances, in the community and in residential establishments.

This chapter will examine the relevance of the Pikler/Gerber approach (referred to in the rest of the chapter as RIE) for young children, their carers, service providers and policy-makers in the UK. We will argue that, in spite of rhetoric, services are rarely child-centered and often fail to support carers or provide protection and optimal development opportunities for our youngest and most vulnerable children. New and proposed policies and legislation are unlikely to improve the situation for children significantly, we suggest below, since they are primarily aimed at structures and organizations rather than supporting changes in our perception and understanding of children, particularly children under three years old. We will argue that it is the most vulnerable children, entitled to family support services in the community, and young children of working parents relying on day care, who could benefit most from consideration of the RIE approach; an approach that promotes a particular kind of relationship between child and parent or carer and is time-rich but resource-modest. First, the current context for services for young children will be explored to reveal the deficits for them of the "market economy" of welfare. Second, we will consider the current emphasis on "poor parenting" and its impact on children and the measures being taken by the state to change parents' practice. Lastly, we will argue that two services in particular, day care and family support services in the community, could benefit from the RIE approach.

The current context for child and family welfare policies in the UK

It has been argued in Chapter 1 that the current welfare policies of the Labour Government are merely a continuation of the developments initiated under the neo-liberal governments beginning with Thatcher's election in 1979 (Burden, Cooper and Petrie, 2000; Randall 2002). Furthermore, despite apparent ideological differences, family welfare policies of both the neo-liberals and New Labour rest on the same construction of the "child." The notional child has a polarized identity: either "victim" or "demon" (Burden, Cooper and Petrie 2000, p.254). Both stereotypes are visible in policy and legislation. Both assume children have little intrinsic competency and are completely dependent on adults for nurture and control, and both are distorted and unhelpful reflections of the needs of children:

> [T]he notion of "child" embedded in policies is constructed in part by socio-economic and cultural factors. The "child" in policy varies from the passive victim of child abuse to the dangerous perpetrator of crime. Neither stereotype offers a helpful insight into the experiences of vulnerable children. (Petrie 2003a, p.123)

Not only are children's needs in general distorted by these stereotypes, but also their individual needs, revealed through their development, attachment and communication, are further masked by the operation of welfare "markets."

Welfare services for young children and their families in the UK, from childcare to primary school education, from health services to social housing are now implemented within a "market" paradigm. This framework does not always support the individual competencies of young children or their capacity for self-directed learning. Their voices are silent in the "market" and their needs frequently secondary to those of adults, whether service-users or service commissioners or providers.

The paradigm for welfare distribution changed significantly from that of the welfare state to welfare "markets," with the implementation of the National Health Service and Community Care Act 1990. Specific structural and financial requirements in relation to services for adults were imposed on local and health authorities. These included separating the management of services from the purchasing of services (purchaser/provider split), and an additional duty to purchase a percentage of services from the independent sector, including the commercial sector. The political agenda underpinning the implementation of the Act was clear and rested on the belief that competition in welfare provision ensures services are more "economic, efficient and effective" (Butcher 2002, p.138) than universal state-provided services. It is accepted by both major political parties that "market" enterprise and the "mixed economy" of welfare is a more equitable and "consumer-sensitive" way of distributing scarce resources to the benefit of society as a whole (Burden *et al.* 2000). The state's historic reluctance to be involved in day care for young children (Jamieson and Owen 2000; Penn 1997; Randall 2002; Riley 1983) has ensured that early years services especially have grown up as a "mixed economy" of voluntary, state and private services.

The Children Act 1989, although under review, is currently the main legislative framework for all protective and support services for vulnerable children, including those entitled to family support services, such as day care, in the community. Although the Act did not impose the same "market" requirements on local authorities for services for children as the NHS and Community Care Act 1990 did for adults, the two Acts were designed to be "consistent and complementary" (Stace and Tunstill 1990, p.1), and it is evident that during the last decade the organization and management of services for children have mirrored those for adults (Petrie and Wilson 1999). *Modernising Social Services* (Department of Health 1998) is the over-arching strategy for social work and social care and sets the agenda for action by prioritizing issues and services for funding. The main services for young, vulnerable children are expected to be those defined as "family support" services. These are often provided by the independent sector as well as statutory agencies, and represent a deliberate shift in policy away from highly interventionist state child protection systems to more supportive community-based services provided by non-statutory organizations from all sectors.

It has been argued, however, that these "markets" for welfare services are not true markets but "quasi-markets" as "consumers"/service-users rarely have purchasing power (Le Grand and Bartlett 1993) and are sometimes (particularly in relation to "family support" services) not willing customers at all (Petrie and Corby 2002). Welfare markets distribute the "child" to service providers as a commodity with associated unit costs. The costs of providing services for children are a primary consideration for service commissioners, usually public bodies such as local authorities and health authorities, in order to ensure "cost-effective" services for "children in need" (Children Act 1989, s.17, cited in Bainham 1990) – the legal passport for state services for vulnerable children. However, although "children in need" are commodified in welfare market transactions between commissioners of services for children and providers, they cannot act as consumers in their own right. They are precluded from being consumers because their entitlement to services is assessed by adults and they are rarely consulted meaningfully as service-users. Older children and young people with purchasing power, however, are firmly placed within the discourse of consumption in markets other than those for welfare services. They are important consumers and are targeted by suppliers of leisure activities, alcohol, clothing and so on. For example, recent research examining young people's views of teenage pregnancy in seaside areas and their rural hinterlands found a clear correlation between the commercial exploitation of young people and their vulnerability to unprotected sex: 'The economic base of the entertainment sectors is dominated by the needs of adults with little concern for the impacts on potentially vulnerable young people, who often experience both economic and sexual exploitation' (Bell et al. 2004).

Furthermore, there is some evidence to suggest that children excluded from participating in the market economy because they are poor may well acquire desirable goods/activities through participation in the "underground economy" (Jordan 1996). For many older children and young people, acquiring visibility in "markets" and becoming desired as consumers by competitive commercial enterprises is perhaps the first time they have had any power or status in the adult world. In these transactions, however, children are often faced with choices they do not have the necessary knowledge, experience or support to negotiate effectively. As far as young children are concerned, their voices are usually silent in the marketplace, and their needs frequently secondary to those of adults, whether service-users, commissioners or providers. It seems, therefore, that the competency of children – to communicate their needs and exercise choice – is only recognized once they have purchasing power. The market paradigm has other deficits for children that have been recognized by government and have stimulated policy and legislative changes.

Fragmenting the service network, in the context of "welfare markets," has had disastrous, sometimes fatal consequences, for some children (Johnson and Petrie 2004; Petrie 2003a; Petrie 2003b). This lack of co-ordination in services was evidenced most recently by the tragic death of Victoria Climbié in 2000 and revealed by the subsequent committee of inquiry chaired by Lord Laming (Laming 2003). The committee's findings and recommendations, although not wholly followed by the government, have underpinned a major piece of re-evaluation of the way in which services for children operate in the UK. A consultation exercise was launched, based on a Green Paper *Every Child Matters* (DfES 2003a) and the subsequent legislation, the Children Bill (HL), was presented to Parliament during the 2003–4 session. The burden of these changes is to ensure that no child can "slip through" the net of services provided by the variety of agencies, state and voluntary, that work with children. There is an attempt, (not the first, it must be said) to place the individual child at the center of the service web and to ensure that service providers work together to meet her needs rather than expecting her and her family to fit into the organizational constraints of each of the many services to which they may be subjected. *Every Child Matters* suggests five "outcomes" for the welfare of children, towards which services should be designed in the future:

- Being healthy: enjoying good physical and mental health and living a healthy lifestyle.

- Staying safe: being protected from harm and neglect and growing up able to look after themselves.

- Enjoying and achieving: getting the most out of life and developing broad skills for adulthood.

- Making a positive contribution: to the community and to society and not engaging in anti-social or offending behavior.

- Achieving economic well-being.

The very different histories, structures and underpinning philosophies of the various service providers involved, across the whole range of health, education and social care in the state, voluntary and private sectors makes the aim of integration towards these outcomes a staggering enterprise which, although intellectually possible, provides an enormous practical challenge. Indeed, as soon as the Green Paper was issued there were calls for it to be less prescriptive in the implementation of its vision. Local authority representatives, for instance, challenged the requirement that they should each appoint a Director of Children's Services to take responsibility, across the whole authority, for implementing the Government's outcomes, and this was acknowledged in the Government's next document *Every Child Matters: The Next Steps*, which was published in April 2004:

> [T]here were concerns that our reforms needed to build in sufficient flexibility to cater for local circumstances and enable a sensitive transition timetable for new arrangements. We have therefore refined our proposals to

ensure we get the right balance between national standards and local flexibility. (DfES 2004)

The Minister of State (Children), at the Department for Education and Skills, Margaret Hodge, admitted in an interview with the *Guardian* newspaper that the original timetable for reform was too ambitious and that changes of such magnitude would take a long time to be realized: " The cultural change has got to be huge, huge…to become the norm, ten years " (Brindle 2004).

These appear to be far-reaching changes in services for children; however, as we indicated earlier, they are mostly structural changes attempting, probably with great difficulty, to alter the way in which adult professionals relate to each other. They will not necessarily alter the way in which they relate to children. It is this essential alteration in our approach to children that is required by the RIE approach and that will, we would argue, be the effective method of improving their life chances in the long run.

One change in the delivery of children's services that does relate more closely to the RIE methodology has been the recognition that they should reflect a "rights" approach. The UK Government is a signatory to the United Nations Convention on the Rights of the Child, but has been severely criticized by the monitoring body for some of the contraventions of the Convention's principles and practices (United Nations Committee on the Rights of the Child 2002). However, there is a growing understanding by child care professionals of the ways in which children's rights can be implemented in service delivery. The movement to consult with children and young people and alter services in order to take account of their needs and wishes has gained momentum over the last few years. The Minister for Children is now instituting her own consultation "Board" in order to listen to the views of young people. In terms of very young children, there is at last a growing understanding of how they too can be listened to and have their wishes and preferences respected. Some of the work that underpins this will be discussed below in the section on day care and working parents.

It should be recognized, however, that the implementation of a "listening" culture is also challenging within a society in which children have traditionally been seen as dependent, or as only commanding respect when they attain purchasing power. This is particularly evident for vulnerable children.

As discussed earlier, complex, affluent societies tend to exclude and constrain very young children, in many ways creating a dependency upon adults that is neither protective nor facilitative of growth. This poor preparation for maturation is rarely noticed until adolescence, however, when the focus of blame is placed firmly on the shoulders of parents and young people themselves.

Family support

The costs and effectiveness of providing family support services compared with statutory child protection services have caused much debate (Petrie 2003a, 2003b). For example, family support and child protection services provided by trained professionals, such as social workers, compared with those provided by community-based programs such as Sure Start local programs. Influential research (DoH 1995), showing that many children were caught up unnecessarily in costly child protection investigations has led to current policy. The *Framework for the Assessment of Children in Need and their Families* (DoH, DfEE, HO 2000) promotes the use of community-based family support services for vulnerable children, where possible, rather than formalized child protection services. However, studies showed that, following the Children Act 1989, day care places for vulnerable children were allocated and paid for by the state primarily in response to adult need and for short periods only – a practice completely at odds with a child's needs for quality care, consistency and stability (Novak *et al.* 1997; Owen and Petrie 1997; Petrie 1995; Statham *et al.* 2001).

The Government's latest initiatives for improving the effectiveness of services for vulnerable children also highlight the importance of family support as the basis of protection:

> Parenting is the most important influence on children and young people's outcomes. We need to shift away from associating parenting support with crisis interventions to a more consistent offer of parenting support throughout a child and young person's life. (DfES 2004)

When the National Childcare Strategy was instituted by the Labour Government in 1997–8, early years services gradually came under the jurisdiction of local education authorities and, at national level, the Department for Education and Employment (DfEE) rather than their traditional home in health and social care (Jamieson and Owen 2000; Randall 2002). This was a popular move with national early years organizations and specialists who had long fought for young children's services to be integrated under one department, rather than split between education and care. They had argued for children's learning to be seen as the central element of universal services. This, it was argued, was more appropriate for children than the one based on a deficit model of day care that assumed most children placed needed social work intervention.

In fact, as we have outlined earlier, day care purchased by the state *had* become reserved for the children of adults with parenting difficulties, and was allocated in a way that did not always support the individual competencies of young children or their capacity for self-directed learning. However, as young children's services have been extended, both through the family support model of Sure Start local programs (DfES 2002) and the growth of full day care for working parents, it may now be less likely that social service departments will purchase day care places for "children in need."

Since policies such as the *Framework for the Assessment of Children in Need and their Families* referred to earlier (DoH, DfEE, HO 2000) emphasize that most vulnerable families would benefit from universal early years services and longer-term community-based support services, it is suggested that this will enable statutory services to reserve their time and funds for the smaller numbers of children needing more intensive support. However, one resulting problem discussed elsewhere (Petrie 2003a, 2003b; Johnson and Petrie 2004) is that children most at risk of harm will undoubtedly be placed in a range of "universal" or community-based services. Staff members in these programs are unlikely to have the detailed knowledge or skills necessary to identify abused children and their families, who may seem initially to be much like any others. It is, of course, focusing on the individual child and their patterns of development and attachment, combined with active listening to non-verbal as well as verbal cues that is the most effective way to protect children.

Although Emmi Pikler and Magda Gerber were remarkably silent about child abuse, and RIE makes little mention of this dimension of "educaring," it can be surmised that this was due to the social context in which they lived and worked, since understanding of child abuse in the US and UK developed significantly from the late 1960s (Petrie and Corby 2002). Of course, as discussed in many of the earlier chapters, Magda Gerber recognized many years ago that education and care were different aspects of the same relationship when she coined the term "educaring." Indeed, if the RIE approach is adopted with infants and toddlers it is possible to understand their world, and any deficits, with great accuracy. Once this is done and avoidable harm revealed, the question of how best to respond may well require the combined efforts of a number of specialists. As has been shown by many studies (DoH 1995), removing a child from his or her family is not always beneficial for the child and, indeed, out-of-family care can also be abusive. However, there is no excuse for failing children, as Victoria Climbié was failed, by relying on adult perceptions of their experiences. We have argued this requires an approach that enables children, however young, to be listened to and to be players in their own lives.

Early years services

Early years services are also essential for working parents, and children's day care has now become a significant element in government economic policies designed to reduce social exclusion/poverty. Poor parents, especially lone parents, are exhorted to enter the labor market as the best way out of poverty for them and their children. Demand has increased, especially for very young children and in impoverished areas; however, the supply is inadequate and existing provision often of poor quality (Craig *et al.* 1999; Owen and Petrie 1997; Penn 1997; Statham *et al.* 2001).

The widespread adoption of the generic term "early years services" has been brought about, as mentioned above, by the sector's long-standing campaign to eliminate the historic care/education split in our services and to create integrated services effectively meeting the learning, health and social needs of young children. Indeed, many early years advocates in many countries, including as we have shown, Magda Gerber and Emmi Pikler, have strived to explain that, particularly for young children, it is impossible to provide for any one of these areas alone. You can neither educate without caring, nor care without promoting children's learning. As Mary Jane Drummond has explained:

> [Y]ou can't turn children's learning off. So the good news is obviously they just keep on learning, however good or bad an environment we provide for them and the equally blindingly obvious bad news is that this means they may be learning the wrong stuff. (Drummond 2002)

Early years services in the UK have, until recently, lacked any form of national financial support. Until 1996, when the Conservative government introduced a voucher scheme to pay for part-time nursery education places for four-year-olds, the extent of provision was determined by the commitment of individual local authorities or the purchasing power of parents. This led to patchy provision, in which some areas had no maintained nursery education or social services day nurseries at all (see Glossary), while others, such as Manchester, Hull and many of the London boroughs, had a strong tradition of both. Equally, voluntary sector provision was dependent on the willingness of local councils to subsidize its costs and support training and advisory services for its staff. Both the voluntary sector, and the growing full-time day care sector in childminding and private day nurseries, were dependent on demand and the ability of parents to pay. Despite a huge surge in the number of places available, this financial profile has changed little. The National Childcare Strategy (Jamieson and Owen 2000; Randall 2002) was based on extending free part-time nursery education to all four, and then three-year-old children whose parents wanted to use it. Full day care is still the responsibility of parents, although the government has put in place measures to help extend availability (for example childminder recruitment incentives, sustainability support for playgroups and innovative project funding for national support organizations). Most notably, the taxation system has been reformed to create a system of tax credits that can be accessed by working parents using regulated day care (see Glossary). Although individual parents still have to pay for their own day care, their capacity to pay has been improved (Jamieson and Owen 2000; Randall 2002).

Quality also has been addressed, because the government recognized that the provision of day care alone would not persuade mothers of young children to enter the labor market. It had to be provision they would be happy to use. Also, the vociferous early years sector, with lobbying skills developed over 40 wilderness years, were not content with a victory solely concerned with increasing places.

The skills of observation and the aim to develop "reflective practitioners" are central to training and qualifications structures in the UK, and are widely agreed to be the foundation of the best quality early childhood care and education in the full range of early years settings (see Glossary). In practice, the implementation of specific curricula for ever-younger children, in an attempt to improve later educational standards, has been considered by many early years specialists to threaten this approach (Pugh 1996). However, as mentioned in Chapter 1, the Foundation Stage curriculum and observation-based profile has been developed to ensure that nursery education principles and practices are implemented for children receiving free nursery education in any setting. Such principles include an emphasis on observation and reflection, and on supporting the child's self-directed learning.

The focus is now shifting to younger children, with a greater understanding of the importance of the earliest years of a child's life. In 2002, Gillian Pugh, the British early years specialist, introduced a new book on the care of babies with the following words:

> In the five years since the study was completed there has been very considerable change in government policy and in levels of provision for children under three, and also in our understanding of the importance of the first three years of life. We now know from research, for example, how quickly the brain is developing during the first twelve months of life, and how susceptible it is to environmental influences. We also know that environmental stress has a negative effect not only on how the brain develops but also on how it functions, and this underlies our capacity to make and sustain relationships. (Edwards 2002)

Pugh referred to a period which did, indeed, see an unprecedented interest in the care and education that is provided for our youngest children, both by their own families and by others. Indeed, as this book goes to print (2004), the UK government is piloting a scheme under which the free nursery education currently provided for three and four-year-olds could be extended to two-year-olds. In the past, the under-threes have sometimes been a neglected age group, thought to be in day care only because their parents worked rather than because the children could derive any positive benefit from it. The good baby was the quiet baby and activities revolved around keeping her clean, fed, safe and rested. However, there have been a number of pioneers in UK early childhood education who have argued for a more sophisticated approach to work with the under-threes. Elinor Goldsmied, for instance, has written and taught for over 40 years, encouraging parents and carers to allow these youngest children to control the pace and nature of their own learning. The most widely known aspect of Goldsmied's work is the "Treasure Basket" (Goldsmied and Jackson 2004). Goldsmied shares with Magda Gerber a stress on the importance of observing the rapidly developing baby and allowing her to dictate the pace and subject of her learning, rather than having this imposed by adults. And it is this recognition of the capacity for learning of the youngest children and the relationship-based approach to meeting their learning needs that is reflected in most of the other national materials which have been produced in recent years.

For instance, two publications from the National Children's Bureau are based on a research study in 1997 that examined the experiences of the increasing numbers of very young children being cared for in day nurseries. The study included in-depth observations of a day in the lives of 15 babies in group day care. *Everyday Stories* (see Glossary) is the transcript of these observations and provides very graphic examples of the way in which pre-verbal children can be handled with little respect for what are sometimes very clearly articulated needs. A practical manual, *Relationships and Learning* (Edwards 2002), uses those observations to illustrate approaches to work with this age group.

Quality in Diversity (Early Childhood Forum 2003) was jointly produced as a learning framework by the 45 member organizations of the Early Childhood Forum, and has particular relevance for this age group. It stands as a testament to the consensus that now exists in the UK early years sector about the principles that should underpin work with the youngest children.

Lastly, the government's response to this interest in the under-threes was *Birth to Three Matters* (DfES 2003), a learning "framework" (not, the authors stress, a curriculum) to support and guide those working with children under three. Professor Lesley Abbott undertook extensive consultation with the early years sector and the conclusions drawn are remarkably similar to those identified by Pikler and Gerber. The central role of observation in determining the abilities and needs of individual children is critical. The role of caring adults is also important, in particular knowing when to intervene to support children's learning, as well as when *not* to intervene, so that children can work things out for themselves or with other children. A quotation from the framework's introductory booklet gives an indication of the ethos:

> Babies and young children need support as they begin a journey of self-discovery from a base of loving and secure relationships with parents and/or a key person. The beginnings of autonomy can be seen in the relationships which exist as babies and young children play and explore alongside a close, attentive, warm and sensitive adult. (DfES 2003, p.8)

All of the above attests to the fact that now, maybe more than ever before, the UK early years sector is united in its understanding of the capacities of babies and the adult dispositions that can develop this potential most fully. In practice, however, as some studies have revealed (National Children's Bureau 2002; Penn 1997), the constraints on early years settings mean that the implementation of improvements in practice is very uneven. The National Day Care Standards, the basis for the annual inspection of registered early years settings by OfSTED (see Glossary), do not provide detailed requirements that would ensure that this approach to children is in place. It is the responsibility of individual settings to improve their practice beyond the minimum standards, and many now do so via specialist quality assurance schemes developed either by their local authorities or by their national professional organization. Such schemes can apply to be endorsed by central government via a national program called Investors in Children.

Apart from those settings that base their practice on one of the specific educational philosophies such as Montessori, Steiner or High/Scope, providers tend to be eclectic, borrowing features of models and approaches that appear to meet their needs. In this situation, it would be possible simply to add RIE to the list of good practice models that settings can draw on. However, this would not be true to RIE practice. Its child-centered approach has led to the development of some practices that may seem alien to a UK audience and that really require us to re-think and re-examine the way in which we work. The recommendation that age groups should be segregated, for instance (see Chapter 4), differs markedly from the practice of childminders in this country and, even in day nurseries, the babies are rarely completely separate from older children. However, in a study of environmental factors in family day care in the US (Weinberger 1998), the providers themselves identified "other children" as the greatest safety hazard for six-month-olds. The partial segregation of babies in "baby rooms" in day nurseries attests to the recognition that this age group needs its own space. Safety, however, is only one of the factors to which RIE practitioners would draw attention. The use of caregiving routines as a central element of learning and development, the time that is given to these and the participation expected of the babies is, although often recommended by child care theorists and trainers, very unusual to find in practice.

Most important overall is the concentrated attention that can be given to the development of the babies. Helen Penn has described very evocatively a nursery in Italy, which had adopted the Pikler approach to its work:

> ...a method has been evolved whereby the staff are *extraordinarily* alert to each child's mood and movements. The attention of the staff is highly focused on the children and it is very unusual to see a child who is being overlooked or ignored. Every nuance of behaviour seems to be followed. More remarkable still than this pitch of vigilance are the controlled responses of the staff. They do not automatically or spontaneously intervene, but make considered choices about how to react to each child in a way that maximizes the child's autonomy, and supports him or her in carrying through and developing chosen tasks... The tenor of the responses by the staff is calm and soothing and considered but they are not inhibited. For instance, at the end of the day when one of the boys, David, a charming friendly bubbly child plays on the slide, slips down it and tumbles onto a soft mat roaring with laughter, then everyone in the room laughs with him, his mood is so infectious... Staff are watchful but do not intervene if they feel the children, even very young children, can deal with the situation by themselves... Some of the happiest and busiest children are here. (Penn 1997, pp. 67–70)

The principles and practices of RIE require this degree of commitment and understanding but, as the contributors to this book have pointed out, they do not require expensive equipment or fancy environments. They do require that practitioners be *interested* in the children and prepared to sit quietly, watching, thinking and learning and modeling that behavior to others (see Figure 8.1). This may seem alien in a culture where we feel we have to keep children busy, and that also we are not earning our pay or being "good" parents, unless we fill their days with activity and their surroundings with color and noise. However, as Catherine Coughlan points out, it is an approach which enables children to be "safe and free," "peaceful and playful."

RIE has been developed, as we hope these chapters have shown, as an integrated and holistic approach to all the environments in a child's life: home, day care, parent support group and so on, and as a way of meeting the needs of children in a range of very different, sometimes challenging, situations. It is in this aspect of the work that its true value lies for children's services in the UK today. It offers the possibility of an approach that makes sense in any service, in any community, for children and for adults, the principles of which can make sense to professionals trained in any of the disciplines now being exhorted to work together to integrate their practice.

Figure 8.1 Practitioners who are interested in children

Conclusion

Pikler and Gerber have demonstrated how to recognize the individuality of the youngest infant, to understand their cues and therefore their needs more accurately. They have shown it is possible to give respect and choice to pre-verbal babies. This way of understanding and interacting with young children does not require expensive equipment or special environments. Parents, day care workers and residential workers have been able to adapt the philosophy to their own conditions to the proven benefit of children. Systematic development of RIE principles and practices, with parents and child care staff in all settings, would meet our current interest in providing services which are holistic and integrated, which recognize and provide for children's individual needs and which allow for the active participation of even the youngest child. If, to borrow the government's phrase, we are truly concerned to ensure that "Every Child Matters", then the potential for developing this work in the UK should be explored.

Glossary

Age groupings
In the US the term "infants/toddlers" covers newborns to two-year-olds, while "pre-schoolers" means children from three to five years old.

Attachment
"Attachment behavior brings infants into close proximity to their main carers. It is within these close relationships that children learn about themselves, other people and social life in general. Young children interact with their parents and other family members and, in so doing, develop an understanding of both themselves and other people." (Howe *et al.*1999, p.10)

Authentic
"An authentic person is one who doesn't have to play a role all the time – someone who is true to himself or herself. If you want an infant to be authentic, you will have to be interested in who that little person really is. That means that the less you assume about the baby, the more you will learn." (Gerber and Johnson 1998, p.71)

California Children and Families State Commission
The Commission was formed following the passage of Proposition 10 in California in 1998, which allowed for the distribution of monies collected from state of California tobacco taxes. It works to implement a comprehensive, integrated program of early childhood health and education services, with an expenditure of over $600 million annually.

Early years "settings"
In this book it can be taken to cover both traditional nursery education settings such as nursery classes in primary schools and maintained and private sector nursery schools, and day care settings such as day nurseries, childminders, pre-schools and play groups, as well as newer institutions such as children's centers.

Educare
"We should educate while we care and care while we educate. To emphasize this, I coined the words 'educarer' and 'educaring' to describe our philosophy." (Gerber 1998, p.1)

Everyday Stories
This is a full transcript of observations of 15 children under three-years-old in day nurseries undertaken by researchers from the National Children's Bureau in 1996–7 and published on the internet in 2002 (www.ncb.org.uk).

James and Joyce Robertson
The filmed observations of **Jane** (17 months, in foster care for 10 days), **Lucy** (21 months, in foster care for 19 days), **Thomas** (2 years 4 months, in foster care for 27 days), and **John** (17 months, in a residential nursery for 9 days) can be obtained from:

> Concord Films Council
> 201 Felixstowe Road
> Ipswich Suffolk
> England
> Tel: +44 (01473) 76012

> New York University Film Library
> 26 Washington Place
> New York NY 10003
> Tel: ++1 (212) 598 2250

Loczy
The large residential home for children under five-years old, established under the directorship of Dr. Emmi Pikler in Loczy Street, Budapest, in 1945. Loczy still provides care for children today under the directorship of Pikler's daughter, Anna Tardos. For further information visit: www.aipl.org/ins-evolution-A.html

The Pikler-Loczy Association of Budapest and the International Emmi Pikler Foundation produce and market video films intended for professional training or for parents. Contact for both:

> Lóczy Lajos utca 3
> 1022 Budapest
> Hungary
> Fax: ++ (36) 1 212 4438
> Email: pikler@matavnet.hu

Videos of the Loczy children can also be obtained from:

> Child Development Media, Inc
> 5632 Van Nuys Blvd
> Suite 286
> Van Nuys CA 91401
> Tel: ++1 (800) 405 8942
> Fax: ++1 (818) 989 7826
> Email: info@childdevelopmentmedia.com

Maintained nursery education

Nursery education which is provided by the local education authority. Social services day nurseries, although originally set up to provide day care for both working parents and children in need were mostly, by the 1980s, available only to vulnerable children. By now most have been closed or converted to centers offering family support services rather than full day care.

Ofsted

Office for Standards in Education, headed by the Chief Inspector of Schools, which inspects all educational establishments, including the full range of early years settings, on behalf of HM government, under relevant legislation and according to national standards. (www.ofsted.gov.uk)

Palmar grasp reflex

"A newborn's hands curl tightly around any object placed in them." (Gonzalez-Mena and Widmeyer Eyer 1993, p.98)

Refueling

This is a common term used in connection with attachment and it refers to the repeated returns that a child makes to an attachment figure for emotional reassurance and comfort while they are exploring their environment. (See also Secure base.)

Regulated day care

This is day care provided by any service sector: statutory, not-for-profit, and for-profit, and regulated by the state under the current provisions in the Children Act 1989. As this book goes to print the government is proposing to introduce a voluntary system under which services previously exempt from regulation, such as nannies, could be approved in order to allow the parents using them to access tax credits.

RIE (Resources for Infant Educarers)

RIE – pronounced "rye" – a non-profit membership organization concerned with improving the care and education of infants established by Magda Gerber and Tom Forrest MD in 1978 in Los Angeles, California. For further information, please contact:

Resources for Infant Educarers
1550 Murray Circle
Los Angeles CA 90026
Tel: ++1 (323) 663 5330
Fax: ++1 (323) 663 5586
Email: Educarer@RIE.org
www.rie.org/

Secure base

A "secure base" refers to the role of the main caregiver in offering the periodic closeness and reassurance desired by the 9-to-12-month-old child developing their autonomy through periodic independent activities. The infant's urge for closeness and attachment is so strong that if the carer doesn't stay close, the child tries to draw the carer to him/her. According to Ainsworth: "The anxious, insecure 9-to-12-month-old may falsely appear more strongly attached to his or her mother than the secure child who can explore in a strange situation using mother as a secure base…in contrast, the insecure child is one who does not explore even when the mother is present. (Fahlberg 1994)

Selective intervention

"Wait! In so many situations, to wait means to allow problems to resolve themselves. Selective intervention means knowing when not to intervene, and this is more difficult than intervening indiscriminately." (Gerber 1998, p.68) (also see Chapter 2).

Tarry time

"This refers to a short space of time which is left to allow a child thinking space between your invitation to them to do something and them responding." (Suskind 1985)

Tonic neck reflex

"When the newborn's head is turned to one side, the arm on that side extends, and the opposite arm flexes, making the baby look like a fencer. This reflex may eventually help the baby use the sides of the body separately." (Gonzalez-Mena and Widmeyer Eyer 1993, p.100)

References

Ainsworth, M.D., Blehar, M.C., Waters, E. and Wall, S. (1978) *Patterns of Attachment: A Psychological Study of the Strange Situation.* Hillsdale, NJ: Erlbaum.

Appell, G. (2003) "Focus on...Emmi Pikler and Loczy." *Children in Europe 5,* September, 27–29.

Bainham, A. (1990) *Children – The New Law: Children Act, 1989.* Bristol: Family Law.

BBC (2002a) "Babies recognise mother's tunes." http://news.bbc.co.uk/1/hi/health/2125207.stm, accessed: 07.13.02.

BBC (2002b) "Babywalkers' stifle development." http://news.bbc.co.uk/1/hi/health/2054550.stm, accessed: 06.21.02.

BBC (2003) "Pupils need far more play time." http://news.bbc.co.uk/1/hi/education/3328823.stm, accessed: 12.23.03.

BBC (2004) "Children start lessons too soon." http://news.bbc.co.uk/1/hi/education/3726039.stm, accessed 05.25.04.

Bell, J., Clisby, S., Craig, G., Measor, L., Petrie, S. and Stanley, N. (2004) *Living on the Edge: Sexual Behaviour and Young Parenthood in Seaside and Rural Areas (LOTE): A Report to the Department of Health.* Hull: Social Research Papers, CASS, University of Hull.

Bowlby, J. (1951) *Maternal Care and Mental Health.* Geneva: WHO.

Bowlby, J. (1973) *Attachment and Loss, Vol II: Separation, Anxiety and Anger.* London: Hogarth Press.

Bowlby, J. (1979) *The Making and Breaking of Affectional Bonds.* London: Tavistock.

Bowlby, J. (1980) *Attachment and Loss, Vol III: Loss, Sadness and Depression.* London: Hogarth Press.

Bowlby, J. (1988) *A Secure Base: Clinical Applications of Attachment Theory.* London: Routledge.

Brindle, D. (2004) "Clash of cultures." *Society Guardian,* 19 May, London.

Bunting, M. (2004) "Are nurseries bad for our kids?" *The Guardian,* 8 July, London.

Burden, T., Cooper, C. and Petrie, S. (2000) *"Modernising" Social Policy: Unravelling New Labour's Welfare Reforms.* Aldershot: Ashgate.

Butcher, T. (2002) *Delivering Welfare* (2nd edn). Buckingham: Open University Press

Children Bill (HL) www.publications.parliament.uk/pa/ld200304/ldbills/035/04035.i-v.html, accessed 03.21.04.

Clarke, A.M. and Clarke, A.D.B. (eds) (1976) *Early Experience: Myth and Evidence.* London: Open Books. New York: Free Press.

Clarke, A.M and Clarke, A.D.B. (2000) *Early Experience and the Life Path.* London: Jessica Kingsley Publishers.

Craig, G., Elliott-White, M., Kelsey, S. and Petrie, S. (1999) *An Audit of Children's Needs in Lincolnshire.* Hull: Policy Studies Research Centre/ULH.

David, M. and Appell, G. (2001) *Loczy. An Unusual Approach to Mothering.* Hungary: Pikler-Loczy Association for Young Children.

Department for Education and Skills (2000) *Curriculum Guidance for the Foundation Stage (3–6 years)*. London: Stationery Office.

Department for Education and Skills (2002) *Sure Start: National Evaluation*. London: Stationery Office.

Department for Education and Skills: Sure Start Unit (2003) *Birth to Three Matters: A Framework to Support those Working with Children Birth to Three Years*. London: Stationery Office.

Department for Education and Skills (2003a) *Every Child Matters*. www.dfes.gov.uk/ everychildmatters/pdfs/EveryChildMattersSummary.pdf, accessed 10.01.03.

Department for Education and Skills (2003b) *Full Day Care: National Standards for Day Care and Childminding*, Standard 2.7.

Department for Education and Skills (2004) *Every Child Matters: The Next Steps*. London: Stationery Office.

Department of Health (1995) *Child Protection. Messages from Research*. London: Stationery Office.

Department of Health (1998) *Modernising Social Services: Promoting Independence, Improving Protection, Raising Standards*. London: Stationery Office.

Department of Health, Department for Education and Employment, Home Office (2000) *Framework for the Assessment of Children in Need and their Families*. London: Stationery Office.

Drummond, M. J. (2002) *Listening to Children Talking*. Transcript of a keynote speech at the Nottingham Early Years conference, National Children's Bureau. www.earlychildhood.org.uk, accessed: 05.26.04.

Early Childhood Forum (2003) *Quality in Diversity* (2nd edn). London: National Children's Bureau.

Edwards, A.G. (2002) *Relationships and Learning*. London: National Children's Bureau.

Eliot, L. (1999) *What's Going On in There? How the Brain and Mind Develop in the First Five Years of Life*. New York: Bantam Books.

Erikson, E.H. (1950) *Childhood and Society*. New York: Norton.

Erikson, E.H. (1965) *Childhood and Society*. Harmondsworth: Penguin.

Fahlberg, V.I. (1994) *A Child's Journey through Placement*. London: BAAF.

Falk, J. (1979) "The importance of person-oriented adult-child relationships and basic conditions thereto." In M. Gerber (ed) (1997) *The RIE Manual: For Parents and Professionals*. Los Angeles: Resources for Infant Educarers.

Falk, J. (1986) "Forty years of Loczy." *Sensory Awareness Foundation Bulletin 14*, Winter 1994, 38–44.

Falk, J. and Pikler, E. (1988) "Data on the Social Adjustment of Children reared in our institution." *Magyar Pszichologiai Szemle 29*, 488–500.

Foundation for the Study of Sudden Infant Death (FSID) (2004) "New advice on reducing the risk of sudden infant death from the Foundation for the Study of Infant Deaths and Department of Health." www.sids.org.uk/fsid/new_advice_ release.htm, accessed: 05.25.04.

Gerber, M. (1971) "Infants' expression – The art of becoming." In I. Jakab (ed) *Psychiatry and Art. Vol 3*. Basel and New York: Karger.

Gerber, M. (1979) "The Loczy model of infant care." In M. Gerber (ed) (1997) *The RIE Manual: For Parents and Professionals*. Los Angeles: Resources for Infant Educarers.

Gerber, M. (1985) *Authentic Infant/Competent Child.* Unpublished lecture notes. Pacific Oaks College.

Gerber, M. (ed) (1997) *The RIE Manual: For Parents and Professionals.* Los Angeles: Resources for Infant Educarers.

Gerber, M. (ed J. Weaver) (1998) *Dear Parent. Caring for Infants with Respect.* Los Angeles: Resources for Infant Educarers.

Gerber, M. (2000)"What is appropriate 'curriculum' for infants and toddlers?" In M. Gerber (ed) *The RIE Manual for Parents and Professionals.* Los Angeles: Resources for Infant Educarers.

Gerber, M. and Johnson, A. (1998) *Your Self-Confident Baby.* New York: John Wiley.

Goldsmied, E. and Jackson, S. (2004) *People under Three: Young Children in Day Care* (2nd edn). London: Routledge.

Gonzalez-Mena, J. and Widmeyer Eyer, D. (1993) *Infants, Toddlers and Caregivers.* London and California: Mayfield.

Gopnik, A., Meltzoff, A. and Kuhl, P. (1999) *How Babies Think: The Science of Childhood.* London: Weidenfeld and Nicholson.

Hobsbawm, E. (1994) *Age of Extremes. The Short Twentieth Century 1914–1991.* London: Abacus.

Howe, D., Brandon, M., Hinings, D. and Schofield, G. (1999) *Attachment Theory, Child Maltreatment and Family Support. A Practice and Assessment Model.* Basingstoke: Macmillan Press.

Hymes, J.L. (1991) *Early Childhood Education: Twenty Years in Review: A Look at 1971– 1990.* Washington DC: National Association for the Education of Young Children (NAEYC).

Jackins, H. (1965) *The Human Side of Human Beings.* Seattle: Rational Island Publishers.

Jamieson, A. and Owen, S. (2000) *Ambition for Change.* London: National Children's Bureau.

Johnson, S. and Petrie, S. (2004) "Child protection and risk-management: The death of Victoria Climbié." *Journal of Social Policy 33,* 2, 179–202.

Jones, C. and Novak, T. (1999) *Poverty, Welfare and the Disciplinary State.* London: Routledge.

Jordan, B. (1996) *A Theory of Poverty and Social Exclusion.* Cambridge: Polity Press.

Laming (2003) *The Victoria Climbié Inquiry: Report of an Inquiry by Lord Laming.* www.victoria-climbie-inquiry.org.uk, accessed 04.10.03.

Le Grand, J. and Bartlett, W. (1993) *Quasi-Markets and Social Policy.* Basingstoke: Macmillan.

Main, M. and Soloman, J. (1986) "Discovery of an insecure-disorganized/disoriented attachment pattern." In T. Brazelton and M. Yogman (eds) *Affective Development in Infancy.* Norwood NJ: Ablex.

Memel, E. (1996) "'Time in' not 'time out'." *Educaring 17,* 2, Spring. Los Angeles: Resources for Infant Educarers.

Money, R. (1992) "Enhancing relationships with babies in a group setting." *Focus on Infancy 4,* Summer. Wheaton, Maryland: Association for Early Childhood International (AECI).

National Children's Bureau (2002) *Everyday Stories.* www.ncb.org.uk, accessed 05.26.04.

Novak, T., Owen, S., Petrie, S. and Sennett, H. (1997) *Children's Day Care and Welfare Markets*. Hull: ULH.

Owen, S. and Petrie, S. (1997) "Who pays the piper? – Aspects of crisis in full-time day care for young children in Britain." In R. Adams (ed) *Proceedings of "Crisis in the Human Services" Conference: Cambridge September 1996*. Hull: ULH.

Parkes, C., Stevenson-Hinde, J. and Marris, P. (eds) (1991) *Attachment across the Life Cycle*. London: Tavistock.

Penn, H. (1997) *Comparing Nurseries*. London: Paul Chapman.

Penn, H. (1999) "How should we care for babies and toddlers? An analysis of practice in out-of-home care for children under three." Occasional Paper 10. Childcare Resource & Research Unit/Center for Urban and Community Studies: University of Toronto.

Petrie, S. (1995) *Day-care Regulation and Support: Local Authorities and Day-care under the Children Act 1989*. London: Save the Children.

Petrie, S. (2003a) "Issues in child abuse." In C. Lyon, with contributions by C. Cobley, S. Petrie and C. Reid Barrister *Child Abuse* (3rd edn). Bristol: Jordan Family Law Publishing.

Petrie, S. (2003b) "Working with families where there are child protection concerns." In M. Bell and K. Wilson (eds) *Practioners' Guide to Working with Families*. Basingstoke: Palgrave Press/Macmillan.

Petrie, S. and Corby, B. (2002) "Partnership with parents." In K. Wilson and A. James (eds) *The Child Protection Handbook* (2nd edn). London: Harcourt.

Petrie, S. and Wilson, K. (1999) "Towards the disintegration of child welfare services." *Journal of Social Policy and Administration 33*, 2, June, 181–197.

Piaget, J. (transl. Margaret Cook) (1975) *The Origins of Intelligence in Children*. New York: International Universities Press.

Pikler, E. (1970) "A Quarter of a Century of Observing Infants in a Residential Center." In M. gerber (ed) (1997) *The RIE Manual: For Parents and Professionals*. Los Angeles: Resources for Infant Educarers.

Pikler, E. (1971) "Learning of motor skills on the basis of self-induced movements." In J. Hellmuth (ed) *Exceptional Infant: Studies in Abnormalities Vol. 2*. New York and London: Brunner/Mazel and Butterworth.

Pikler, E. (1994) "Peaceful babies – contented mothers." In M.E. Roche (ed) *Sensory Awareness Bulletin 14*, Muir Beach, CA: Sensory Awareness Foundation.

Pinker, S. (1994) *The Language Instinct: The New Science of Language and Mind*. London: Penguin.

Pinto, C. (2001) "Supporting competence in a child with special needs: One child's story." *Educaring 22*, 2, Spring. Los Angeles: Resources for Infant Educarers.

Psychological Corporation (1969) *Manual for the Bayley Scales of Infant Development*. New York: Psychological Corporation.

Pugh, G. (1996) *Four Year Olds in Schools: What is Appropriate Provision?* London: NCB.

Randall, V. (2002) "Childcare in Britain, or, how do you restructure nothing?" In S. Michel and R. Mahon (eds) *Child Care Policy at the Crossroads*. London: Routledge.

Reggio Children (1996) *The Little Ones of Silent Movies/I Piccolissimi del Cinema Muto*. Reggio Emilio, Italy: Reggio Children.

RIE (1984) *Seeing Infants with New Eyes* (video). Los Angeles: Resources for Infant Educarers.

Riley, D. (1983) *War in the Nursery: Theories of the Child and the Mother.* London: Virago.

Rushton, A. (2003) *The Adoption of Looked After Children. A Scoping Review of Research.* London: SCIE.

Rutter, M. (1975) *Helping Troubled Children.* Harmondsworth: Penguin.

Rutter, M. (1981) *Maternal Deprivation Reassessed.* Harmondsworth: Penguin.

Sidebotham, P. (2001) "An ecological approach to child abuse: A creative use of scientific models in research and practice." *Child Abuse Review 10,* 2, 311–320.

Spitz, R.A. (1945) "Hospitalism: An inquiry into the genesis of psychiatric conditions in early childhood". *The Psychoanalytical Study of the Child 1,* 53–79.

Stace, S. and Tunstill, J. (1990) *On Different Tracks. Inconsistencies between the Children Act and the Community Care Act.* London: Voluntary Organisation Personal Social Services Group.

Statham, J., Dillon, J., Moss, P. (2001) *Placed and Paid For. Supporting Families through Sponsored Day Care.* London: Stationery Office.

Sutton, C. (1994) *Social Work, Community Work and Psychology.* Leicester: British Psychological Society.

Suskind, D. (1985) "The importance of tarry time." *Educaring 6,* 4, Fall. Los Angeles: Resources for Infant Educarers.

United Nations Committee on the Rights of the Child (2002) *Consideration of Reports Submitted by States Parties under Article 44 of the Convention, Concluding Observations of the Committee: United Kingdom of Great Britain and Northern Ireland.* www.unhchr.ch/html/menu2/6/crc/doc/co/United%20KingdomCO2.pdf, accessed 05.30.04.

Ward, S. (2000) *Baby Talk.* London: Century.

Weinberger, N. (1998) "Making a place for infants in family day care". *Early Education and Development 8,* 1, January.

Williams, F. (1995) *Social Policy: A Critical Introduction.* Cambridge: Polity Press.

Wilson, K., Petrie, S. and Sinclair, I. (2003) "A kind of loving – A model of successful foster care: Part 2." *British Journal of Social Work 33,* 991–1003.

Subject Index

abilities *see* capacities, of infants

accreditation *see* training program, RIE

adoption 29

adults
  comfort of 88–89
  interactions between 94, 98, 102
  treating in same way as children 114–15, 123

age grouping 24, 65, 70, 75, 77–78, 138–39, 141

agencies (US) 72

aggressive behavior 50

Alternative Payment Program (APP), California 71

assessment 31, 32

Associate, RIE 124–25

attachment theory 141
  childcare policy (UK) 20–22
  classification system 22
  relationships 23
  secure attachments 93

attention, of carer 25, 46, 48, 49, 65, 74, 75, 97, 110, 139

attention span 15, 65, 73

authenticity 141
  "authentic" infants 94–95, 100, 110
  emotions, freedom of 60
  relationships 14, 27, 53, 56
  role-playing RIE 115–17, 123
  security and affiliation 61–62

sensitive observation 66–67

autonomy 39, 49, 90

awakening 42, 74, 89

baby-bouncers 38, 73

bathing 25, 29, 39, 85

bed 40

bedtime 44, 89

benefits, for carers *see* compensation

birth 67

birth family 28, 32

Birth to Three Matters (DfES 2003) 137–38

blame 41, 102, 133

body control 61, 62, 73, 97
  see also gross motor development

bottle 41, 49, 62, 74, 87, 89

brain development 136

breakdown, placement 29–30

budgets 80, 108

California Children and Families State Commission 107, 141

California Work Opportunity and Responsibility to Kids (CalWORKS) 71

capacities, of infants
  cognitive/social/emotional 32
  independent play 65
  language acquisition 63, 74, 79
  relationships 20, 28, 136
  respect for 30, 37–38, 40–41, 49, 57–58, 96, 138
  self-directed learning 16, 62, 68, 128, 134, 137, 138

social learning 43, 66
  see also gross motor development

care/education split 133–35

care regime 18, 23, 24, 30

caregivers, qualities of 90

caregiving activities
  diapering 39, 57, 66, 75, 87
  feeding/mealtimes 62, 74–75, 87–89, 110f
  value of 21, 49, 74–75

caregiving routines 15, 48, 49, 87–89, 122, 139

carer, use of term 19

categories, family 84

center size (US) 70, 77, 80

cerebral palsy 78

certification *see* training program, RIE

child abuse, and RIE 134–35

child-centered approach 14, 16, 18, 21, 30, 49, 52, 127, 138

Child Development Block Grant (CDBG) 71

child development theory 22

child protection (UK) 129, 133–34

childcare policy (UK) 20–22
  see also family support services

childminders 69, 136, 138, 141

Children Act (UK) (1989)
  children "in need" 31, 129–30, 133
  "equal concern" 14

Children Bill (UK) 131

Children's Health Council 26, 53

Climbié, Victoria 130, 134

climbing 63, 73, 78, 97, 98

cognitive development 20,
    22, 30, 32, 39, 48, 60,
    61, 63, 64, 67, 123,
    125, 131
collaborative model of
    development 93–94
collective responsibility 31,
    33
commitment
    to family 84
    to quality care 90–91
communication, with infant
    50, 53
    see also relationships
Community Care Act (UK)
    (1990) 128, 129
Community Care Licensing
    70–71
compensation 48, 71, 72,
    81
competence see capacities, of
    infants
conflict resolution 49–50
consciousness, altered state
    of 89
Conservative government
    31, 128, 135
consultation exercises 131,
    138
consumers, children as 130
continuity 24, 25, 86–87
control see body control
cooperative relationships
    32, 44, 57, 64, 66, 75,
    94, 114
costs 71–72, 80, 107
crime 20, 71, 128
crying 40, 41–42, 49, 50,
    60
cultures, differing 13, 25,
    31, 38, 43, 121
curriculum, and learning
    89–90
    see also Early Years
        "Curriculum" (RIE)

Daily Discoveries Child
    Development Center,
    Maryland 86
day nurseries 135, 137,
    138, 139, 141
Dear Parent: Caring for Infants
    with Respect (Gerber) 72,
    108
deficit model, of day care
    133
Demonstration Infant
    Program (DIP) 26–27,
    52, 53
Dempster Bequest Fund 10
Department for Education
    and Employment 133
dependence see
    interdependence
deprivation see attachment
    theory
development, collaborative
    model of 93–94
diapering 39, 57, 66, 75,
    87
discipline
    choice within
        boundaries 44
    consistency 43–44
    as "educaring" 45
    meanings of 42–43
    parent–infant guidance
        classes 100
    parents' expectations
        43
    reasonable age-
        appropriate rules 43
    rules, modeling 45
    saving face, allowing for
        44
dismorphia 64
diversity 93, 94
drives 60, 67, 89, 122
Dubnoff School, Pilot Infant
    Program 25, 52

earliest years (UK)
    interest in 136–37

learning frameworks
    137–38
observations, use of
    137
relationship-based
    approach 137
early childhood education
    4, 12, 53, 69, 72, 81,
    109
Early Childhood Forum
    137
Early Years "Curriculum"
    (RIE)
    communication 53
    "educaring" 52
    everyday experience,
        incorporating 54
    independence, and
        interdependence
        57–62
    optimal health, fostering
        54
    out-of-home care,
        growth of 52–53
    predictability 54
    respectful relationships
        52, 54, 56–57
    SBIC 51–52
    self-awareness 54
    self-initiated activity 54
early years services (UK)
    capacities of infants,
        understanding 138
    care/education split
        135
    as "mixed economy"
        129
    national financial
        support 135–36
    observation skills 136
    quality 136
    "reflective practitioners"
        136
    universal 133–35
    working parents 135
early years settings (UK)
    136, 138–39
eco-systemic framework 21

Educaring (newsletter) 14, 35
educaring 45, 48–50, 52, 134, 141
education
  care/education split 133–35
  collaborative model of development 93
  early childhood 4, 12, 53, 69, 72, 81, 109
  higher 15
  mainstream 26, 51
  maintained nursery 135, 143
  pre-school (UK) 30, 31–32, 52, 53, 72, 77–79, 83, 90, 141
effectiveness, evidence of
  Loczy 27–30
  RIE 30–31
empowerment, of
  parents/carers 16, 26, 107
environment
  cognitively challenging 64
  comfort of adults 88–89
  emotionally nurturing 39, 63, 64, 91
  peaceful and playful 73, 81
  physically safe 63–64, 72–73, 81f, 88, 97
"equal concern" 14
equipment 9, 60, 63, 65, 86, 139, 140
ethnic diversity 12, 94, 127
Europe, influence of Pikler's work in 18–19
Every Child Matters: The Next Steps (DfES 2004) 131–32
Every Child Matters (DfES 2003) 131
Everyday Stories 137, 141
evidence-based practice 13

excellence 15, 83, 84
  see also quality care
exclusion *see* social exclusion
expenses 80
experimentation 73, 74
eye–hand coordination 60

families, involvement of 76, 84
family day care (US)
  agencies 72
  compensation 72, 80–81
  costs and subsidies 71–72, 80
  licensing procedure 70–71
  providers 72
  small *versus* large centers 70, 77, 80
  state regulation 70
  training/experience requirements 71
family members 44, 45, 80
family support services (UK)
  "child", stereotypical notions of 128
  child protection 129, 133–34
  Loczy/RIE approach, benefits of 32, 33
  needs of child, as central 131
  "rights" approach 132–33
  service integration, task of 131–32
  state-funding 31–32
  vulnerable children 129
  welfare "market" paradigm 128–29
  welfare outcomes 131
  see also early years services
fatalities 73, 130
feeding 62, 74–75, 87–89, 110f
fees *see* costs

fine motor development 29, 49, 125
food *see* feeding
foster care 10, 19, 29, 142
Foundation Stage curriculum 32, 136
Framework for the Assessment of Children in Need and their Families (DoH, DfEE, HO) 21, 133, 134
frameworks
  discipline 43, 44
  learning 137–38
  Loczy regime 24
  parent–infant guidance classes 97–102
  see also Framework for the Assessment of Children in Need and their Families
freedom
  of choice 44
  of emotion 60, 62
  to explore 65–66
  of movement 25, 26, 62, 73, 79, 100
  in play 60
  in problem solving 61
  in relationships 55, 60, 68
funding *see* state funding

government *see* childcare policy; Conservative government; early years services; family support services; New Labour government; state funding
government programs 12, 32
grants *see* state funding
gross motor development
  developmental stages 58–59, 64
  educaring 49
  independence, building 39, 58–60, 63

Loczy, effectiveness of
22–23, 29
respectful relationship,
building 56–57
RIE, effectiveness of 30
self-initiated behaviors,
trust in 63
group care, pros and cons of
48
group sizes/ratios 80,
85–86

harm, from day care 13–14
Head Start (US) 52
health and safety 71, 80
helpers/assistants 50, 77,
80
high chairs 40, 87
High/Scope 138
higher education 15
household activities 79

independence 57–62
independent sector
organizations 12
infant–caregiver interaction
13, 29, 80, 87, 99, 100,
110
see also caregiving
activities; caregiving
routines; feeding
infant–infant interaction
49, 61, 65, 67, 75–76,
110
injuries 71, 73
insecurity 13, 22, 41
inspection 13, 70–71, 138
institutional care 20, 28,
29, 32
integration, service 16, 131
intellectual development see
cognitive development
interaction
adult 94, 98, 102
infant–caregiver 13,
29, 80, 87, 110
infant–infant 49, 65,
67, 75–76, 110

non-verbal 63
respectful 18, 26, 27,
74, 75
social 57, 61
stressful 32
interdependence
cooperative relationships
32, 57
innate competence 57
respect 58
security and affiliation
62
intimacy 75–81
Investors in Children 138

key worker 25

language development 63,
74, 79
leadership 15, 90, 91
learning
and curriculum 89–90
frameworks 137–38
parental 46–48
self-directed 16, 62,
68, 128, 134, 137,
138
social 43, 66
licensing procedure (US)
70–71
lifestyle 26, 38, 90, 121,
131
limits, setting 67
Loczy model 142
age grouping 24
application of 12, 13,
14, 17, 25, 27,
32–33, 53, 56
continuity of care 24,
25
effectiveness, evidence
of 27–30
establishment of 18
gross motor
development 22–23
individual needs,
meeting 24
influence of 36–37

optimal development
23
Pikler's goals 22–23
poor resources 13, 24
positive outcomes 23
principles of 23–24, 54
staffing approach 23
UK context, relevance to
13, 19
lone parents see single
parents
Los Angeles 10, 12, 25, 70,
118
Los Angeles City College
program 108
love 48, 50, 90

mainstream education 26,
51
maintained nursery
education 135, 143
management 15, 84, 91,
129
manipulation 44, 98
market see welfare "market"
paradigm
materials 27, 44, 48, 86,
89, 90, 115, 137
maternal deprivation see
attachment theory
"maternal" versus
"professional"
relationship 19
maturation 132
mental health 20, 26, 131
mentor, role of
adults, treating in same
way as children
114–15, 123
lessons learned 123–24
mentor/mentee
relationship 113
messenger is also
message 117–18
needs of infants,
understanding 122
relationships, lesson in
121

respectful collaborative
relationships 122
role-playing RIE
115–17, 123
social realities,
limitations of 122
their vision of the child,
understanding
119–21, 124
time, for understanding
RIE 122–23
what they want to
know, versus
"teaching" 118–19,
123–24
milestones, developmental
56, 60, 63, 73
Minister of State (Children)
132
Modernising Social Services
129
monitoring 132
moral development 61
mothers 14, 52, 53, 72, 99,
106, 108, 136
see also attachment
theory
motor development see gross
motor development; fine
motor development
movement, freedom of 38,
73, 114

nappy-changing see
diapering
National Association for
Family Child Care (US)
72
National Association for the
Education of Young
Children (US) 53
National Childcare Strategy
(UK) 12, 133, 135–36
National Children's Bureau
11, 137, 138, 141
National Curriculum (UK)
32

National Day Care
Standards (UK) 138
National Health Service and
Community Care Act
(UK, 1990) 128–29
National Methodological
Institute for Residential
Nurseries see Loczy
national support
organizations 136
needs of child,
understanding 21, 18,
122, 131
Neighborhood Child Care
Program (California) 72
neo-liberal governments
128
New Labour government
31, 128, 133
newborns 40–41, 43, 67,
83, 99, 104, 141
non-statutory organizations
129
nursery education (UK) 32,
135, 136, 137

observation
and commenting 74,
103
early years 136, 137
gross motor
development 62–63
parent–infant guidance
classes 16, 104–5,
109
sensitive 66–67, 95–97
OfSTED 85, 138, 143
organizations 12, 129, 136
out-of-home care (US)
52–53
outdoor activities 78–79

pacifiers 42
palmar grasp reflex 64, 143
parent–child interaction see
infant–caregiver
interaction
parent education 11, 13

parent–infant guidance
classes
authentic relationships
94–95, 100, 110
competence, of infants
96, 106
costs of 107
demonstration 56, 57,
95, 99–100, 109
discipline 100
human development,
collaborative model
of 93–94
infant- and
adult-oriented classes
46
infant–infant interaction
110
infant-initiated
separation 99–100
long-term learning
46–48
observation 15–16, 46,
94–96, 104–5, 109,
110
parent support 18,
45–46, 94
physical environment
97
reciprocity 109
respect 100
selective intervention
95, 96
self-initiated exploratory
behavior 111
snack time 45, 100
staff team 98–99
student feedback 109
trust 96–97
vulnerable children, and
their families 107–8
parents/carers
concerns of 103
discussions/
disagreements 106,
110
empowerment of 16,
107

fears, freeing from 103
respect for 102–3,
106–7
transformation of
105–6
participants, children as 22,
26, 39, 58, 66
pay *see* compensation
pedagogy, child-centered
16
pediatrician 12, 14, 18, 26,
27, 36
personality development 60
philosophy
child-centered 13
Loczy 25
RIE 15, 27, 37, 48, 51,
53, 58, 84, 94, 95,
96, 100, 109,
113–25
physical environment *see*
environment
Pikler-Loczy Association of
Budapest 142
placement breakdown
29–30
play, uninterrupted 22, 60,
65, 73–74, 97
playgroups 136
policy *see* childcare policy;
early years services;
family support services
poor early care, outcomes
from 20–22
positive qualities,
recognizing 119–21
potential, of children 29,
32, 84, 109, 138
poverty 12, 20, 27, 31, 33,
135
pre-school education (UK)
30, 31–32, 52, 53, 72,
77–79, 83, 90, 141
pre-verbal babies 52, 56,
137, 140
predictability 54
preventive approach 26, 94

primary caregiver 64, 85,
99
primary schools 16, 128,
141
private day nurseries 11,
13, 52, 135
private sector 108, 129,
131, 141
problem-solving skills 26,
61, 64, 95, 100, 119
"professional as expert"
model 93
professional relationship 19
providers (US) 72
proximity-seeking 21
psychological development
20, 29, 57
psychologists 14, 36
public funding *see* state
funding

qualifications *see* training
program
quality assurance schemes
(UK) 138
quality care 9
caregiving routines
87–89
commitment to 90–91
continuity 86–87
curriculum and learning
89–90
excellence 15, 83, 84
family, commitment to
84
groups and ratios
85–86
importance of 13
management
responsibilities for
91
placement breakdown
29–30
"relationship-based"
philosophy 83–84
staff team 90–91
Quality in Diversity (Early
Childhood Forum) 137

ratios, children/provider
80, 85
record-keeping, data from
27–28
recruitment 80, 81, 136
"reflective practitioners"
136
refueling 61, 105, 111,
143
regulated day care 14, 136,
143
regulations 14, 48, 53, 70,
71, 80, 85
relationship-based
philosophy 83–84
relationships
attachment theory 23
authenticity 14, 27, 53,
56
capacity for 20, 28,
136
cooperative 32, 44, 57,
64, 66, 75, 94, 114
freedom in 55, 60, 68
respectful 12, 52, 53,
54, 55–57, 122
and trust 22, 26, 54
Relationships and Learning
(Edwards) 137
residential care 20, 25, 31
residential institutions 14,
17, 18, 19, 36, 53, 127,
142
Resources for Infant Carers
see RIE
respect
capacities of child
37–38, 41, 62–63,
69, 73, 95, 96, 103
childcare practices
41–45
children as subjects 37
consistency 67
environment 63–64
independence and
interdependence 58
infant–infant interaction
65

interdependence 58
letting go 37–38
modeling 26
for parents/carers
102–3, 106–7
relationships 12, 52,
53, 54, 55–57, 122
sensitive observation
66–67
uninterrupted play
64–65
see also mentor, role of
respectful interaction 18,
26, 27, 74, 75
retention, of staff 80, 81
RIE (Resources for Infant
Carers) 143
background 12, 13, 14
child, understanding
10–11
curriculum 15
effectiveness of 30–31
establishment of 27
organization 10
principles into practice
14–16
skepticism about 9–10
see also Early Years
"Curriculum" (RIE)
"rights" approach 132–33
risk 13, 26, 52, 107, 134
rolling 58–59, 73, 104
routines 44, 48, 49, 54, 77
caregiving 15, 87–89,
122, 139
safety, of physical
environment 63–64,
72–73, 81f, 88, 97
SBIC see South Bay Infants
Center
schools 18, 31, 107, 108
scientific studies 22, 23,
149
seats 38, 40, 47, 78
secondary caregiver 85
secure attachments 93
see also attachment
theory

secure-base effect 21, 144
Seeing Infants with New Eyes
69–70
selective intervention 26,
95, 96, 139, 144
self-esteem 22
self-expression 16, 96
self-initiated activity 15,
25, 26, 54, 60, 62, 66,
68, 111
self-soothing activities
41–42, 49, 89
sensitivity 21, 93
separation behavior 21, 22
see also attachment
theory
service commissioners 16,
128, 130
service-users 16, 128, 129,
130
services
integration of 16, 131
universal 129, 133,
134
see also early years
services; family
support services
settings 141
siblings 77, 107
single parents 10, 11, 31,
80, 108
sitting 56, 59, 63, 73, 99
sleep 32, 38, 42, 44, 45,
73, 76, 77, 89, 103
snacks 45, 99, 100
social care 129, 131, 133
social exclusion 12, 31,
135
social interaction 57, 61
Social Services 70, 129,
135
social work 16, 129, 133
social workers 115, 133
South Bay Infants Center
(SBIC) 51–52, 53–54
special educational needs
19, 25, 26, 106

spontaneity 23, 29, 62,
139
sports-casting 61
staff team 90–91, 98–99
standards 85, 132, 136,
138
state funding 83, 84,
107–8
costs and subsidies (US)
71–72, 80
family support services
(UK) 13, 31 32,
135–36
state government (US) 70
state regulation (US) 70
see also licensing
procedure (US)
status, of family day care
48, 72, 80
statutory sector 12, 129,
133, 134
staying calm 50
stress 32, 103, 136
subjects, children as 24, 37,
54
subsidies see state funding
substitute family care 29,
30
sucking 41–42
support
parent 18, 45–46, 94
see also family support
services
Sure Start programs (UK)
11, 12, 133, 134
swings 40, 73, 114

tantrums 61
tarry time 66, 144
tasks 15, 24, 65, 75, 87,
139
taxation 31, 107, 136, 141
teaching 30, 38, 39, 47,
49, 57, 73, 88, 89, 90,
93, 108, 113–26
teenage pregnancy 130
Thatcher governments 31,
128, 135

thumb-sucking 41–42
"time in" 64
time-rich approach 16, 128
toileting 52, 67, 85
tonic neck reflex 59–60,
    144
toys 40, 60, 64, 74, 97, 98
training program, RIE 70,
    72
    alliance of RIE certified
        teachers 124, 125
    three-part certification
        10, 124–25
transitions 71, 75
"Treasure Basket"
    (Goldsmied and
    Jackson) 137
trips 79
trust
    capacities of child
        37–38, 41, 62–63,
        69, 73, 95, 96, 103
    parent–infant guidance
        96–97
    relationships 22, 26,
        54, 113–26

under-threes *see* earliest years
    (UK)
United Nations Convention
    on the Rights of the
    Child 132
universal services 129, 133,
    134

versatility, of RIE approach
    14, 17, 25, 127
voluntary sector 129, 131,
    135
voucher scheme, for
    part-time nursery
    education 135
vulnerable children
    empowerment, of
        parents 107
    family welfare policy
        (UK) 129

government-funded
    programs 107–8
parental feedback 108
private funding 108

wages *see* compensation
wagons 78–79
walkers 38, 40, 73
walking 61, 63, 64, 73,
    105
welfare "market" paradigm
    16
    children as consumers
        130
    legislative underpinning
        128–29
    "quasi-markets"
        129–30
    service coordination,
        lack of 130–31
    "underground economy"
        130
well-being 13, 23, 33
whole child, focus on 49
women, as primary carers
    20–21
workforce 20, 32, 33, 52,
    53, 91
working parents 19, 103,
    108, 127, 132, 134,
    135, 136